PENGUIN REFERENCE

**THE STATE OF WAR AND PEACE ATLAS**
third edition

Dan Smith is Director of the International Peace
Research Institute, Oslo (PRIO). With Michael Kidron, he
coauthored the first two editions of this atlas, published
in 1983 and 1991.

Kristin Ingstad Sandberg was a Research Assistant at
PRIO from 1994 to 1996.

Pavel Baev is a Senior Researcher at PRIO, and former
Section Head at the Institute of Europe, Moscow. His
most recent book is *The Russian Army in a Time of
Troubles*.

Wenche Hauge is a Researcher at PRIO, where her
studies focus on the causes and dynamics of armed
conflicts.

PRIO was founded in 1959, when it was one of the
world's first centres of peace and conflict research.
An independent institute with an international staff, it
has an outstanding reputation for research on the
causes, dynamics and consequences of conflict and of
peace.

Also in this series:

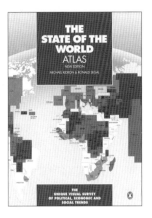

**THE STATE OF THE WORLD ATLAS**
fifth edition
by Michael Kidron and Ronald Segal

**THE STATE OF
WOMEN IN THE WORLD ATLAS**
second edition
by Joni Seager

# THE STATE OF
# WAR AND PEACE
# ATLAS

new revised third edition

Dan Smith

with
Kristin Ingstad Sandberg
and
Pavel Baev and Wenche Hauge

International Peace Research Institute, Oslo

PENGUIN
REFERENCE

PENGUIN REFERENCE

Published by the Penguin Group
Penguin Books Limited, 27 Wrights Lane,
London W8 5TZ, England
Penguin USA Inc., 375 Hudson Street,
New York, New York 10014, USA
Penguin Books Australia Limited,
Ringwood, Victoria, Australia
Penguin Books Canada Limited, 10 Alcorn Avenue,
Toronto, Ontario, Canada M4V
Penguin Books (NZ) Limited, 182-190 Wairau Road,
Auckland 10, New Zealand
Penguin Books Limited, Registered Offices:
Harmondsworth, Middlesex, England


First published 1997
10 9 8 7 6 5 4 3 2 1

Penguin Reference hardcover  0-670-10007-2
Penguin Reference paperback  0-14-051373-6

Produced for the Penguin Group by
Myriad Editions Limited, 32 Hanway Street,
London WIP 9DD

Edited and co-ordinated for Myriad Editions by
Anne Benewick and Candida Lacey
Graphic design by Corinne Pearlman
Text design by Pentagram Design Limited
Maps created by Angela Wilson for
Line + Line Limited, Thames Ditton, Surrey

Printed and bound in China
Produced by Mandarin Offset Limited

# CONTENTS

There are times when anything seems possible, even that the world will become more democratic and more peaceful. That was how it seemed as the Cold War came to a close at the end of the 1980s and start of the 1990s, and with it the arms race that had been run and the local wars that had been fought in its name.

Yet if much changed with the end of the Cold War, much remained the same. We still live on an armed and warring planet, in which power is concentrated in few hands, and human ingenuity is devoted to perfecting modern weaponry. Freedom is still sacrificed to power and people continue to die in wars that are fought only to decide which unrepresentative group of people should control a given area. And the privileged, prosperous and peaceful parts of the world remain largely unaware of what is going on. Although some wars and the tragedies they create receive intense coverage from the international news media, most of today's wars continue to be fought in countries about which the major news organizations know little and care less.

The end of the Cold War did not resolve all the problems it created. In wars that have proven stubbornly difficult to end in Angola and Cambodia, and in the environmental hazards created by testing and stockpiling nuclear weapons, the Cold War continues to cast a long shadow.

The end of the Cold War also led to new problems. Political adjustment to change in the international order always takes time. Much of the process has been a matter of high politics, diplomatic manoeuvre and the redeployment of economic resources. But some adjustment has been violent. Wars have started in Europe and the former USSR that would not have been fought had the Cold War continued.

Global change has brought new dangers as well as new opportunities and the store of human wisdom available to face those challenges is not noticeably greater today than it was at the height of the Cold War.

Whatever else may be said about the Cold War, it created a world that was familiar for several decades. The shape of international politics in the 1990s contains much that people find hard to grasp because it is new, uncertain and still evolving. To chart this changing world for the third edition of this atlas, I have attempted to

provide information on a global, regional and even local scale. There is far less emphasis than in the two previous editions on the global system of power and much more on the peculiarities of local and regional conflicts. In the sense that a global system of power broke down and no new, similarly global system has yet emerged to replace it, this partial shift in focus from the general to the particular reflects what has happened to world politics.

Many people have helped in the preparation of this book. Not much moves without money, and I am glad to acknowledge that a grant from the Ford Foundation and contracts from the United Nations Development Programme have helped make it possible to gather the data on which this atlas is based. I have had to turn to a wide range of people and organizations not only for information but also for helping to interpret complex, incomplete and often contradictory data. They are listed in the Acknowledgements on page 11 where they receive a collective and heartfelt thank you. Others deserve more specific mention.

Foremost among them is Kristin Ingstad Sandberg. She has been an outstanding research assistant and without her the book would not have been possible. She displays a rare combination of diligence and creativity, logic and imagination, along with a readiness to learn from others where she can and teach herself when she must. Among her talents, as many of those listed in the Acknowledgements would confirm, she has developed an uncannily persuasive telephone manner. Most of all, she was fun to work with and in the grim process of compiling a compendium of war, atrocity and generalized inhumanity, the capacity to find corners of humour and pleasure is an essential human quality.

It has also been a pleasure to have two other colleagues at the International Peace Research Institute, Oslo, working with me on this edition. Pavel Baev and Wenche Hauge offered their particular research skills and regional expertise in developing several of the map manuscripts, and as well as thanking them for their work, I want to thank them for their patience and good humour as I went back to them for niggling additional data.

Anne Benewick, Candida Lacey and Corinne Pearlman at Myriad Editions have been a creative concept, design and editorial team. Anne and Candida have also coordinated the project with considerable shrewdness. They have been full of encouragement when that was what I needed, which was occasionally, and full of patience when that was what they needed, which, regrettably, was often.

Michael Kidron invited me to help him on the first edition, which was published in 1983. We worked together on the second edition, which came out in 1991.

He stepped aside for this edition and contented himself with offering ideas, creative insights and encouragement I am in his debt for his most recent contributions, and despite the labour he caused me grateful beyond words for getting me into this in the first place.

Dan Smith
Oslo, July 1996

# ACKNOWLEDGEMENTS

I would not have started – and would certainly not have been able to finish – the work on this atlas if I were not confident that I could get help (and sometimes get it repeatedly) from a wide variety of friends, colleagues and contacts. All those named here have been generous with their time and knowledge but, of course, none is responsible for the use to which I have put their expertise.

Tony Allan, School of Oriental and African Studies, London; Anna Lena Andrews, Swedish Save the Children, Stockholm; Tom Argent, US Committee for Refugees, Washington D.C.; Günther Bächler and Franziska Bacher, Swiss Peace Foundation, Berne; Carmel Bedford, The Rushdie Committee, London; Jacob Bercovitch, University of Canterbury, New Zealand; Gry Berg, Norwegian Water Resources and Energy, Oslo; Tore Bjørgo, Norwegian Institute of Foreign Policy (NUPI), Oslo; Tony Borden, Institute for War and Peace Reporting, London; Rachel Brett, Quaker UN Office, Geneva; Simon Burrowes, Department of Economic Development, Belfast; Rajan Chelliah, Tamil Coordinating Committee, Oslo; Karen Colvard, Harry F. Guggenheim Foundation, New York; Andrew Cooper, UN Department of Humanitarian Affairs, New York; Louise Doswald-Beck, International Committee of the Red Cross, Geneva; Lena Endresen, Institute for Applied Social Science (FAFO), Oslo; Cynthia Enloe, Clark University, Massachusetts; Lawrence Fabry, International Committee of the Red Cross, Geneva; Lynn Failing, UN Relief and Works Agency for Palestine Refugees in the Near East (UNRWA), Vienna; E. J. Flynn, UN Centre for Human Rights, Geneva; Bill Frelick, US Committee for Refugees, Washington D.C.; Greenpeace, Norway; Greenpeace International, Netherlands; Dave Harris, Africa Centre, London; Lorna Harris, St. Andrews University, Scotland; Albert E. Jongman, University of Leiden, Netherlands; Michael Kidron; Ole Kopreitan, The Norwegian Campaign No To Nuclear Weapons; Jostein Leiro, The Norwegian Foreign Affairs Department, Oslo; Robert Mandel, Lewis and Clark College, Oregon; Erin McCandless, Minority Rights Group, London; Bill McSweeney, Irish School of Ecumenics, Dublin; Petter Næss, American Embassy, Oslo; Steen Nørskov, Information Newspaper, Copenhagen; Peter Quande, Norwegian Peoples Aid, Oslo; Magne Raundalen, Centre for Crisis Psychology, Bergen; Leif Røssaak, Israeli Embassy, Oslo; Joni Seager, University of Vermont, Burlington; Margareta Sollenberg, Department of Peace and Conflict Research, Uppsala University, Sweden; Tatyana Termacic, International Criminal Tribunal for the Former Yugoslavia, Den Haag; Valery Tishkov, Institute of Ethnology and Anthropology, Moscow; Joan Todd, Northern Ireland Statistics and Research Agency, Belfast; Arne Tollan, Norwegian Water Resources and Energy (NVE), Oslo; Jon Martin Trolldalen, Center for Environmental Studies and Resource Management (CESAR), Oslo; Peter Wallensteen, Department of Peace and Conflict Research, Uppsala University, Sweden; Paul Wilkinson, St. Andrews University, Scotland; Mr. Wimmer, UN Department of Humanitarian Affairs, New York; Arthur H. Westing, Westing Associates, Putney, Vermont; Dorothea Woods, Geneva; Geir Øvensen, Institute for Applied Social Science (FAFO), Oslo; Geir Øvstus, The Bellona Foundation, Oslo.

## PRIO
All my colleagues at PRIO have been stimulating and indirectly helpful while I have been preparing this atlas, but the following have been of direct assistance with information, research findings and assistance in interpreting difficult data: Bayo Adekanye, Magne Barth, Synnøve Eifring, Victoria Ingrid Einagel, Tanja Ellingsen, Franz Gundersen, Kristian Berg Harpviken, Nora Ingdal, Jan Tore Savic Knutsen, Nada Merheb, Ketil Volden.

## LIBRARIES
Scholars need libraries and I have needed and deeply appreciated the help of the following libraries and staff: Anne Lindefjell and Anette Kragh, Library of the UN Association in Oslo; Anne C. Kjelling, Elisabeth S. Kresen, Inger Guri Fløgstad, Library of the Nobel Institute in Oslo; Arve Ryan and Aliya Paulsen, the Library of the University of Oslo; staff of the library at the Institute for Geography, University of Oslo; staff of the information office of the Norwegian Agency for Development Cooperation; staff of the library of the Norwegian Broadcasting Corporation; Department of Information, the British Embassy, Oslo; US Library of Congress.

Part One: **THE DYNAMICS OF WAR**

1991
65 wars

1992
66 wars

1990
54 wars

ANNUAL NUMBER
OF WARS
*1989-95*

1993
57 wars

1989
47 wars

1994
60 wars

1995
55 wars

**War is:**
**• open armed conflict**
**• about power or territory**
**• involving centrally organized fighters and fighting**
**• with continuity between clashes**

**From 1990 to 1995, 70 states were**
**involved in 93 wars which killed**
**five and a half million people.**

# 1 THE RED HORSE

**'And there went out another horse that was red: and power was given to him that sat thereon to take peace from the earth, and that they should kill one another: and there was given unto him a great sword.'**

The Revelation of St John the Divine: chapter 6 verse iv

Most of today's wars are civil wars. The dominant pattern is of rumbling conflicts that, from time to time across a decade, erupt viciously into action. There are exceptions, such as the massacre in Rwanda in 1994, the wars of Yugoslavia's disintegration from 1991 to 1995, or the swift campaign of the Gulf War in 1991. It is the exceptional cases that the western news media covers. For the most part, modern war resembles a slow torture. Often, only one region of a country is involved.

Today's wars offer few triumphs and only rarely produce disasters that take a whole nation to despair and destruction. They simply continue. More than half the wars of the 1990s lasted for over five years, two fifths lasted for more than ten years and a quarter for more than twenty. The action is often fitful. These wars lack clean outlines. It is difficult to know when they have begun and if or when they have ended. Open declarations of war are rare. Ceasefires and peace agreements are more often made than honoured. Premature announcements of victory or peace are common.

Most wars are fought with relatively low technology weapons. The laser guided, video recorded weapons of the Gulf War of 1991, the cruise missiles that turn right at the traffic lights — these are the weapons of a completely different kind of war from what has been happening in Burma, Liberia and Peru or even Bosnia-Herzegovina. Long range artillery and air power may be used but most of the killing is at close quarters.

Most of the casualties are civilians. At the beginning of the twentieth century between 85 and 90 percent of war deaths were military. By the Second World War, over half of all war deaths were civilians, including victims of death camps, massacres and bombing raids on cities. And at the end of the twentieth century, about three quarters of war deaths are civilians.

Through war, one group imposes its will upon another. War is about power and politics. Variously, wars are fought for national independence, to control territory or natural resources, to take over the government in the name of justice, national unity or some other cause — or to prevent these things from happening. Wars are fought to protect the identity of a nation or an ethnic group, sometimes by resisting an alien power, sometimes by crushing another group. But the causes for which people and states fight are not the same as what causes them to fight. The situation that creates the need to achieve a goal by force of arms grows from many factors — economic, historical, political, cultural.

Not only do wars have multiple causes, but what keeps a war going is often different from what started it. What began as a struggle against a tyrant may continue as a dispute over the fruits of victory. At that point, war starts to become self reproducing and eventually a way of life. It continues for no better reason than inertia. After a while, making peace is harder than carrying on fighting. This is true for the leaders whose only claim on power and prestige is their control of a few hundred fighters. It can be equally true for the fighters themselves, who know that no normal life is waiting for them back in their homes that have been destroyed. When this happens, war is no different from banditry.

It is part of the tragedy of many countries that, even then, fighting forces can recruit new members and stay in the field. They get recruits by a variety of means. Some guerrilla groups terrorize peasants into joining up, or into giving them their children. It is a form of protection payment by a village, even if it may bring reprisals from government forces. They also find volunteers among the impoverished, the miserable, the starving, the people with no other prospects, with no hope and no reason for hope.

When the conditions of ordinary life are a violence, a violent response is hardly surprising. The form it takes depends on many things, from personal psychology through family circumstance, to social pressure and political opportunity. Each person joins the guerrillas for individual reasons, but in a context of desperation that leads to desperate choices.

In these conditions, in the soil from which armed conflict grows, there is a strong link between war and the resources needed for a decent life, or, rather, the lack of resources and their unfair distribution.

In much of the world, it is difficult for ordinary people to find the basic minimum of economic and environmental necessities — a living wage, clean water, good soil. When a privileged elite defends its too large share of too few resources, the link is created between poverty, inequality and the abuse of human rights. The denial of basic freedoms — to organize, to express yourself, to vote, to disagree — forces people to choose between accepting gross injustice and securing a fairer share by violent means. As conflict unfolds, the political leaders that emerge often find that the easiest way of mobilizing support is on an ethnic basis. Thus do the various causes of conflict weave in and out. War will end only if, and when, and where its causes are removed.

# 2 CONFLICTS OF INTEREST

**Armed conflict is concentrated among the world's poorer countries.**

RICH AND POOR *mid 1990s*
Gross National Product (GNP) per person
US dollars

| | |
|---|---|
| $695 | low income countries |
| $2,785 | lower middle income |
| $8,625 | upper middle income |
| | high income |

Armed conflict in the 1990s

interstate war

civil war

RUSSIA

KAZAKHSTAN

MONGOLIA

UKRAINE

TURKEY

GEO
AZER
UZBEKISTAN
KIRGISTAN
TURKMEN
TAJ

CHINA

N KOREA
JAPAN
S KOREA

CIS
SYRIA
LEB
ISRAEL
JOR
IRAQ
KUWAIT
AFGHANISTAN

PACIFIC
OCEAN

IRAN

QATAR
BAHRAIN
UAE

PAKISTAN

NEPAL
BHUTAN

SAUDI ARABIA

OMAN

EGYPT

INDIA

B
DESH

BURMA

TAIWAN

LAOS

THAILAND

VIETNAM

ERITREA
YEMEN

DJIBOUTI

JORDAN

CAM

PHILIPPINES

ETHIOPIA

SOMALIA

UGANDA

KENYA

SRI LANKA

BRUNEI

MALAYSIA

SINGAPORE

TANZANIA

COMOROS

INDONESIA

PAPUA
NEW
GUINEA

MALAWI

MADAGASCAR

ZAMBIA

ZIMBABWE

MOZAMBIQUE

AUSTRALIA

GREENLAND
(Den)

CANADA

RUSSIA

KAZAKHSTAN
MONGOLIA

UNITED STATES
OF AMERICA

TURKEY

CHINA

JAPAN

NEW
ZEALAND

ALGERIA
LIBYA

IRAN

INDIA

SUDAN

THE DEBT BURDEN *mid 1990s*
National debt as a
proportion of GNP percentages

ZAIRE

BRAZIL

INDONESIA

AUSTRALIA

60%    heavily indebted countries

15%    medium debt

low debt

no data

**17**

# 3 REGIMES AND RIGHTS

**The worse the abuses of human rights, the greater the probability of war.**

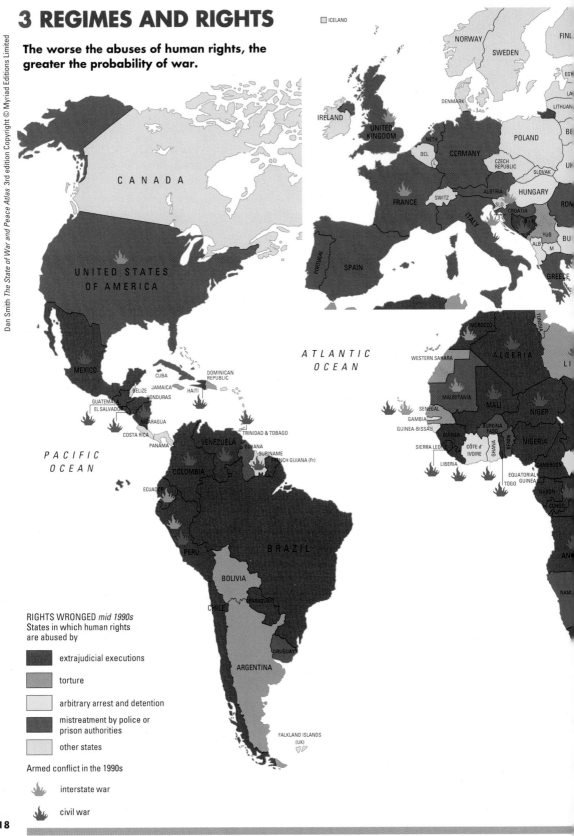

RIGHTS WRONGED *mid 1990s*
States in which human rights
are abused by

- extrajudicial executions
- torture
- arbitrary arrest and detention
- mistreatment by police or prison authorities
- other states

Armed conflict in the 1990s

- interstate war
- civil war

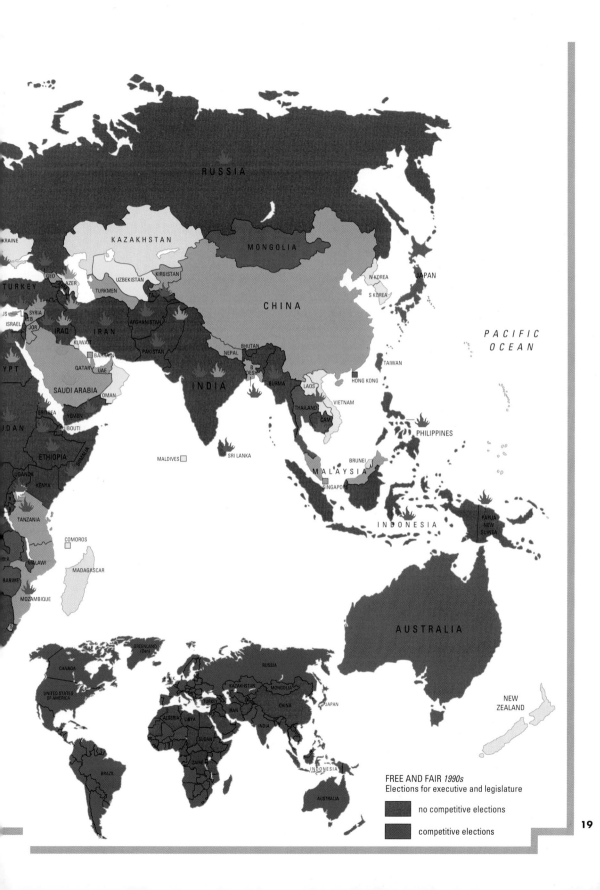

RUSSIA

UKRAINE

KAZAKHSTAN

MONGOLIA

N KOREA

JAPAN

GEO
AZER
TURKEY
UZBEKISTAN
KIRGISTAN
S KOREA

US
SYRIA
LEB
ISRAEL
JOR
IRAQ
KUWAIT
TURKMEN
TAJ
AFGHANISTAN
IRAN

CHINA

PACIFIC
OCEAN

BAHRAIN
QATAR
UAE
PAKISTAN
BHUTAN
NEPAL
TAIWAN

YPT
SAUDI ARABIA
OMAN
INDIA
B
DESH
BURMA
LAOS
HONG KONG

ERITREA
YEMEN
DJIBOUTI
THAILAND
VIETNAM

JDAN
SUMALIA
MALDIVES
SRI LANKA
CAM
PHILIPPINES

ETHIOPIA
BRUNEI

UGANDA
KENYA
MALAYSIA

SINGAPORE

TANZANIA
COMOROS
INDONESIA
PAPUA
NEW
GUINEA

IA
MALAWI
MADAGASCAR

BASWE
MOZAMBIQUE

AUSTRALIA

CANADA
GREENLAND
(Den)

RUSSIA

UNITED STATES
OF AMERICA
KAZAKHSTAN
MONGOLIA
JAPAN

NEW
ZEALAND

TURKEY
IRAN
CHINA

ALGERIA
LIBYA
SUDAN
INDIA

BRAZIL
ZAIRE
INDONESIA

AUSTRALIA

FREE AND FAIR *1990s*
Elections for executive and legislature

no competitive elections

competitive elections

**19**

**Ethnic groups sometimes live together in peace. Often, they are at war.**

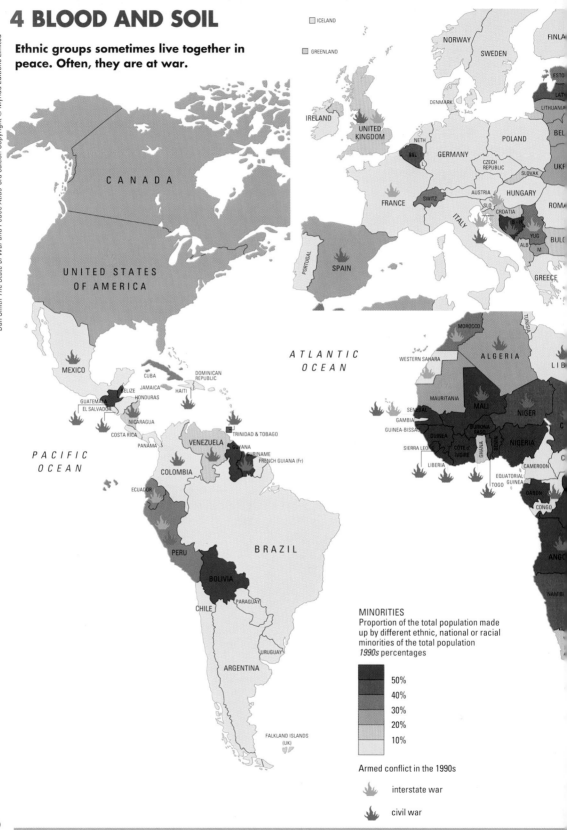

MINORITIES
Proportion of the total population made up by different ethnic, national or racial minorities of the total population
*1990s* percentages

- 50%
- 40%
- 30%
- 20%
- 10%

Armed conflict in the 1990s

- interstate war
- civil war

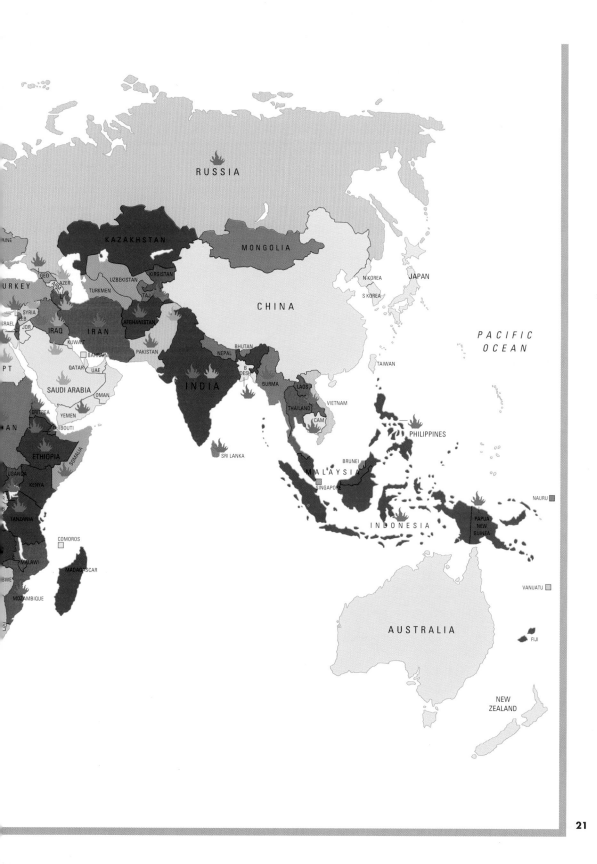

RUSSIA

KAZAKHSTAN

MONGOLIA

N KOREA

JAPAN

S KOREA

UKRAINE

GEO

AZER

UZBEKISTAN

KIRGISTAN

ARM

TURKMEN

TAJ

URKEY

SYRIA

LEB

ISRAEL

JOR

IRAQ

KUWAIT

IRAN

AFGHANISTAN

CHINA

TAIWAN

PACIFIC
OCEAN

BAHRAIN

PAKISTAN

NEPAL

BHUTAN

QATAR

UAE

B
DESH

SAUDI ARABIA

OMAN

INDIA

BURMA

LAOS

AN

ERITREA

YEMEN

THAILAND

VIETNAM

CAM

DJIBOUTI

PT

PHILIPPINES

ETHIOPIA

SOMALIA

UGANDA

SRI LANKA

BRUNEI

KENYA

MALAYSIA

NAURU

SINGAPORE

TANZANIA

COMOROS

INDONESIA

PAPUA
NEW
GUINEA

MALAWI

MADAGASCAR

VANUATU

IBWE

MOZAMBIQUE

AUSTRALIA

FIJI

NEW
ZEALAND

Terrorism is warfare by another name — the low level, low intensity use of violence for political ends.

**Germany 1992-94** Skinheads and neo Nazis carry out over 5,000 attacks on foreigners. Seventeen die.

**Oklahoma 1995** 167 killed by truck bomb allegedly planted by right wing extremists.

**New York 1993**
6 killed and 1,000 injured by World Trade Center bomb.

**Buenos Aires 1994**
Car bomb at Israel Argentine Friendship Association kills 100 and injures 200.

**INTERNATIONAL TERRORIST INCIDENTS**
*1990-94*

- 100 incidents
- 10 incidents
- no international terrorist incidents
- deaths from international terrorism *numbers given*
- domestic terrorism

Dan Smith *The State of War and Peace Atlas* 3rd edition  Copyright © Myriad Editions Limited

RUSSIA

4

KAZAKHSTAN

MONGOLIA

CHINA

N.KOREA

S KOREA

JAPAN

11

**Tokyo 1995** Aum Shinrikyo cult kills 11 in subway nerve gas attack.

UKRAINE
OL

50

45

UZBEKISTAN

KIRGISTAN

TURKMEN

TAJ.

45

GEO
AZER

TURKEY

40

PRUS

SYRIA
DEB

ISRAEL

JOR

IRAQ

1

KUWAIT

BAHRAIN

190

73

GYPT

QATAR

UAE

4

SAUDI ARABIA

OMAN

IRAN

1

1

AFGHANISTAN

5

PAKISTAN

42

NEPAL

BHUTAN

B
DESH

31

INDIA

BURMA

TAIWAN

*PACIFIC
OCEAN*

LAOS

VIETNAM

THAILAND

3

CAM

PHILIPPINES

22

ERITREA

2

YEMEN

DJIBOUTI

UDAN

1

ETHIOPIA

SOMALIA

SRI LANKA

295

MALAYSIA

SINGAPORE

BRUNEI

4

**Colombo 1996** Tamil Tigers kill 87 with hotel bomb.

UGANDA

R
B

KENYA

TANZANIA

INDONESIA

PAPUA
NEW
GUINEA

MBIA

MALAWI

MADAGASCAR

MBABWE

MOZAMBIQUE

5

S

AUSTRALIA

bombs
692

armed
attacks
580

INTERNATIONAL TERRORISM
Number of incidents by type
*1990-94*

assassinations
258

kidnapping
171

other
114

NEW
ZEALAND

# 6 THE DEATH TOLL

There were about five and a half million war deaths in the first half of the 1990s. Three quarters of them were civilians, including a million children.

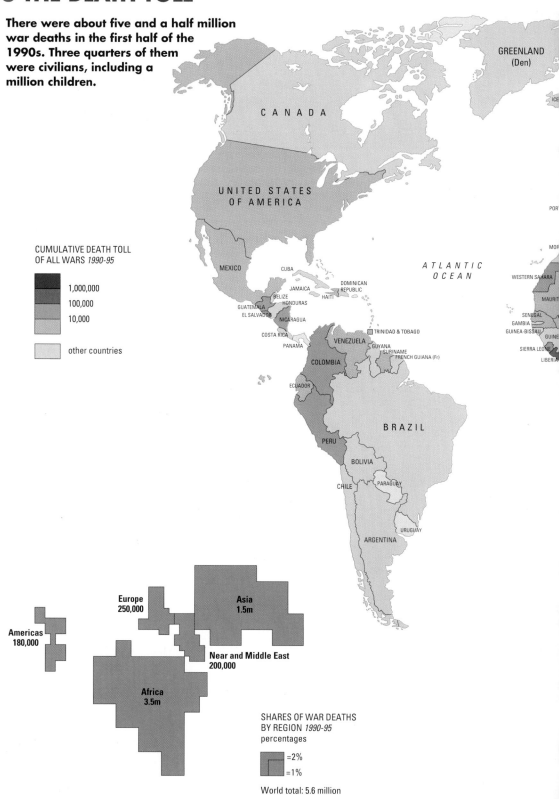

CUMULATIVE DEATH TOLL
OF ALL WARS *1990-95*

- 1,000,000
- 100,000
- 10,000

other countries

GREENLAND
(Den)

ICE

CANADA

UNITED STATES
OF AMERICA

POR

MOR

ATLANTIC
OCEAN

WESTERN SAHARA

MEXICO

CUBA

MAURIT

JAMAICA

DOMINICAN
REPUBLIC

SENEGAL

BELIZE

HAITI

GAMBIA

HONDURAS

GUINEA-BISSAU

GUATEMALA

GUINE

EL SALVADOR

NICARAGUA

SIERRA LEONE

COSTA RICA

TRINIDAD & TOBAGO

LIBERIA

PANAMA

VENEZUELA

GUYANA

SURINAME

COLOMBIA

FRENCH GUIANA (Fr)

ECUADOR

BRAZIL

PERU

BOLIVIA

CHILE

PARAGUAY

URUGUAY

ARGENTINA

Europe
250,000

Asia
1.5m

Americas
180,000

Near and Middle East
200,000

Africa
3.5m

SHARES OF WAR DEATHS
BY REGION *1990-95*
percentages

- =2%
- =1%

World total: 5.6 million

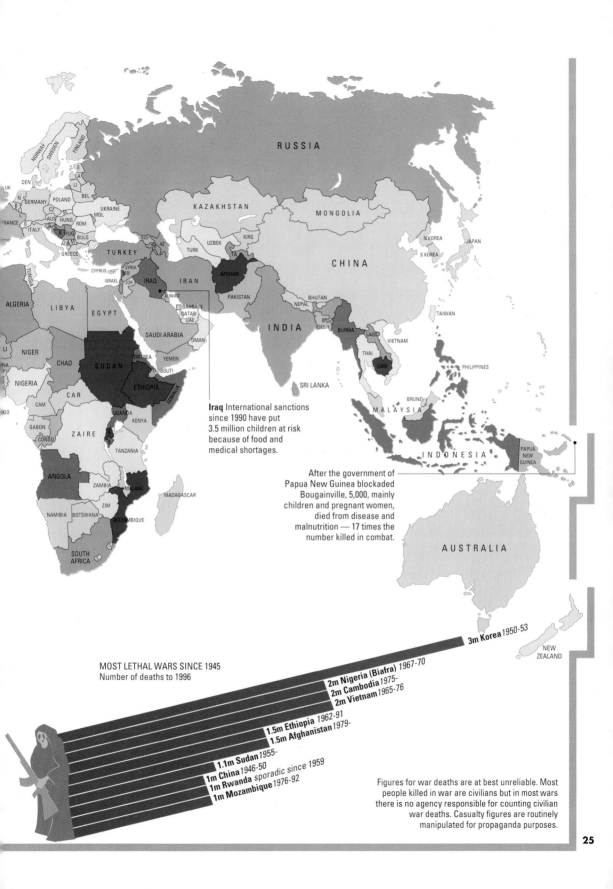

**Iraq** International sanctions since 1990 have put 3.5 million children at risk because of food and medical shortages.

After the government of Papua New Guinea blockaded Bougainville, 5,000, mainly children and pregnant women, died from disease and malnutrition — 17 times the number killed in combat.

MOST LETHAL WARS SINCE 1945
Number of deaths to 1996

3m **Korea** 1950-53

2m **Nigeria (Biafra)** 1967-70
2m **Cambodia** 1975-
2m **Vietnam** 1965-76

1.5m **Ethiopia** 1962-91
1.5m **Afghanistan** 1979-

1.1m **Sudan** 1955-
1m **China** 1946-50
1m **Rwanda** sporadic since 1959
1m **Mozambique** 1976-92

Figures for war deaths are at best unreliable. Most people killed in war are civilians but in most wars there is no agency responsible for counting civilian war deaths. Casualty figures are routinely manipulated for propaganda purposes.

# 7 FEAR AND FLIGHT

**There are almost 40 million refugees worldwide. Just over half are refugees in their own countries. Women and children are more likely to be made refugees then men.**

UNSAFE
States contributing to world population of refugees and displaced people
*1995* percentages

states of 3% or over: percentage given

☐ =1.0%
☐ =0.1%

Internally displaced people as a proportion of all refugees

- all refugees are internally displaced
- more than 50% are internally displaced
- less than 50% are internally displaced
- all refugees have fled abroad

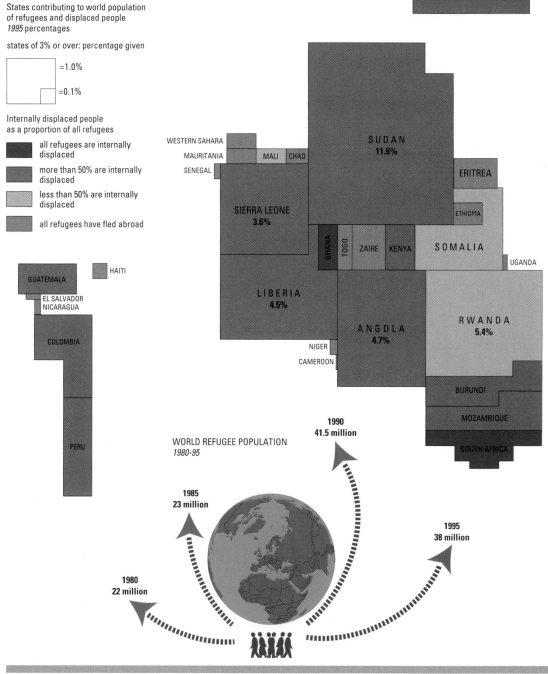

CROATIA

YUGOSLAVIA

BOSNIA-HERZEGOVINA
**5.8%**

WESTERN SAHARA
MAURITANIA
SENEGAL
MALI
CHAD
SUDAN
**11.6%**
ERITREA
ETHIOPIA
SIERRA LEONE
**3.6%**
GHANA
TOGO
ZAIRE
KENYA
SOMALIA
UGANDA

HAITI

GUATEMALA
EL SALVADOR
NICARAGUA
LIBERIA
**4.5%**
ANGOLA
**4.7%**
RWANDA
**5.4%**

COLOMBIA
NIGER
CAMEROON
BURUNDI

MOZAMBIQUE

PERU
SOUTH AFRICA

WORLD REFUGEE POPULATION
*1980-95*

1990
41.5 million

1985
23 million

1995
38 million

1980
22 million

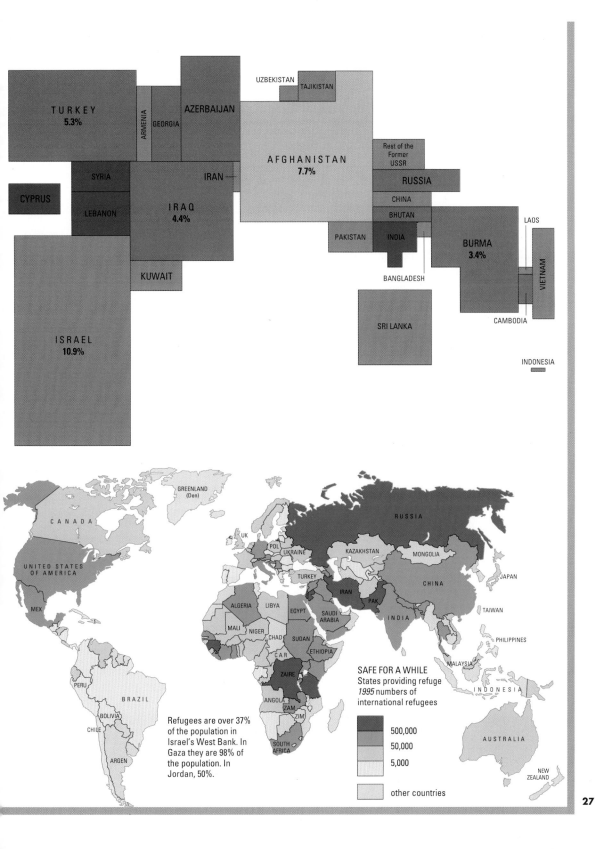

UZBEKISTAN

TAJIKISTAN

TURKEY
5.3%

ARMENIA GEORGIA

AZERBAIJAN

AFGHANISTAN
7.7%

Rest of the
Former
USSR

SYRIA

IRAN

RUSSIA

CYPRUS

LEBANON

IRAQ
4.4%

CHINA

BHUTAN

PAKISTAN

INDIA

BURMA
3.4%

LAOS

KUWAIT

BANGLADESH

VIETNAM

ISRAEL
10.9%

SRI LANKA

CAMBODIA

INDONESIA

GREENLAND
(Den)

CANADA

RUSSIA

UK

POL

UKRAINE

KAZAKHSTAN

MONGOLIA

JAPAN

UNITED STATES
OF AMERICA

TURKEY

IRAN

PAK

CHINA

TAIWAN

MEX

ALGERIA

LIBYA

EGYPT

SAUDI
ARABIA

INDIA

PHILIPPINES

MALI

NIGER

CHAD

SUDAN

PERU

CAR

ETHIOPIA

MALAYSIA

BRAZIL

ZAIRE

INDONESIA

BOLIVIA

ANGOLA

CHILE

ZAM

ZIM

Refugees are over 37%
of the population in
Israel's West Bank. In
Gaza they are 98% of
the population. In
Jordan, 50%.

SOUTH
AFRICA

ARGEN

**SAFE FOR A WHILE**
States providing refuge
*1995* numbers of
international refugees

500,000

50,000

5,000

other countries

AUSTRALIA

NEW
ZEALAND

27

# 8 LETHAL LEGACY

Over 100 million landmines lie in the soil, with the power to kill or maim for decades. A single US dollar will buy a landmine; clearing it can cost $300 to $1,000.

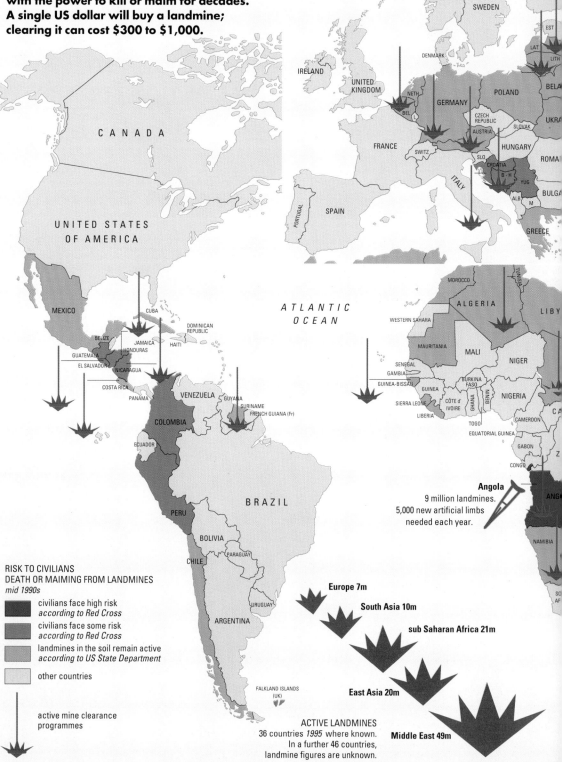

**Angola**
9 million landmines.
5,000 new artificial limbs needed each year.

**RISK TO CIVILIANS**
**DEATH OR MAIMING FROM LANDMINES**
*mid 1990s*

- civilians face high risk *according to Red Cross*
- civilians face some risk *according to Red Cross*
- landmines in the soil remain active *according to US State Department*
- other countries

active mine clearance programmes

Europe 7m
South Asia 10m
sub Saharan Africa 21m
East Asia 20m
Middle East 49m

**ACTIVE LANDMINES**
36 countries *1995* where known.
In a further 46 countries, landmine figures are unknown.

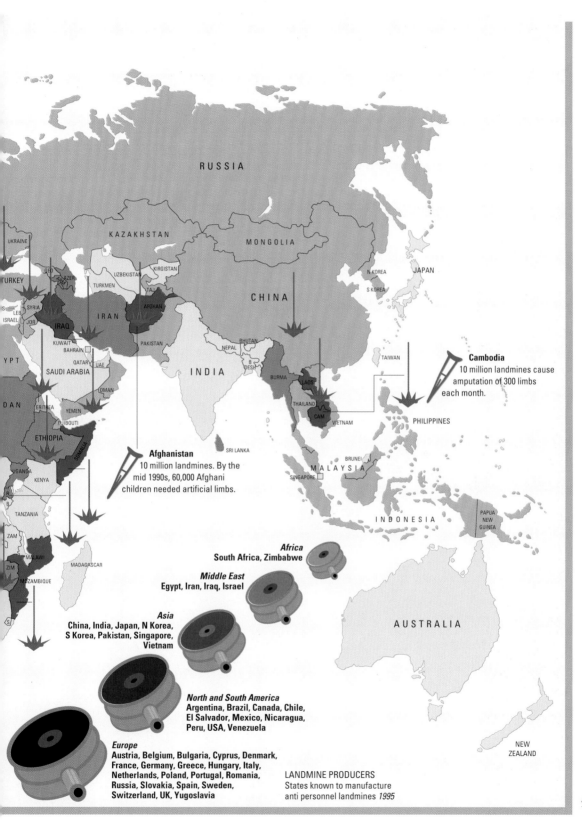

RUSSIA

UKRAINE

KAZAKHSTAN

MONGOLIA

TURKEY

GEO
ARM AZER
TURKMEN
UZBEKISTAN
KIRGISTAN
TAJ

KIRGISTAN

N KOREA

JAPAN

S KOREA

S
LEB
ISRAEL
SYRIA
JOR

IRAQ

IRAN

AFGHAN

CHINA

YPT

KUWAIT
BAHRAIN
QATAR UAE

SAUDI ARABIA

OMAN

DAN

ERITREA

YEMEN

DJIBOUTI

ETHIOPIA

SOMALIA

UGANDA

KENYA

TANZANIA

ZAM

MALAWI

ZIM

MOZAMBIQUE

MADAGASCAR

PAKISTAN

NEPAL

BHUTAN

B
DESH

INDIA

BURMA

THAILAND

LAOS

CAM

VIETNAM

SRI LANKA

TAIWAN

PHILIPPINES

BRUNEI

MALAYSIA

SINGAPORE

INDONESIA

PAPUA
NEW
GUINEA

AUSTRALIA

NEW
ZEALAND

**Cambodia**
10 million landmines cause
amputation of 300 limbs
each month.

**Afghanistan**
10 million landmines. By the
mid 1990s, 60,000 Afghani
children needed artificial limbs.

*Africa*
South Africa, Zimbabwe

*Middle East*
Egypt, Iran, Iraq, Israel

*Asia*
China, India, Japan, N Korea,
S Korea, Pakistan, Singapore,
Vietnam

*North and South America*
Argentina, Brazil, Canada, Chile,
El Salvador, Mexico, Nicaragua,
Peru, USA, Venezuela

*Europe*
Austria, Belgium, Bulgaria, Cyprus, Denmark,
France, Germany, Greece, Hungary, Italy,
Netherlands, Poland, Portugal, Romania,
Russia, Slovakia, Spain, Sweden,
Switzerland, UK, Yugoslavia

LANDMINE PRODUCERS
States known to manufacture
anti personnel landmines *1995*

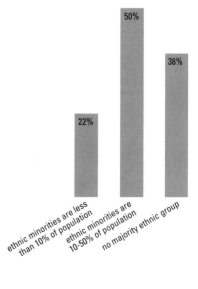

WAR *1990-95*

Percentage of countries experiencing war,
grouped by extent of ethnic diversity

50%

38%

22%

ethnic minorities are less
than 10% of population

ethnic minorities are
10-50% of population

no majority ethnic group

How can one talk to a nine year old child about the fact
that his father shot his best friend?

I asked him for his own explanation, and he looked right
in my eyes and said, 'I think they have been poisoned,
they have been drinking something that has been
poisoning their brains.' But he suddenly added, 'But now
they are all poisoned, so I'm sure it is in the drinking
water, and we really have to find out how to clean the
polluted water reservoirs.' When I asked him if children
were as much poisoned as adults he shook his head and
said, 'No, not at all. They have smaller bodies, so they
are not drinking so much, so they are less contaminated,
and I have discovered that small children and babies
who mostly drink milk, they are not poisoned at all.'

I asked him if he had ever heard the word politics.
He almost jumped and looked at me and said, 'Yes.
That's the name of the poison.'

*Magne Raundalen, a Norwegian psychologist, describes
a session with 'Ivan' from Bosnia-Herzegovina*

# 9 THE DISINTEGRATION

**Between 1991 and 1995, during the wars of Yugoslavia's disintegration, over 150,000 people were killed, three million became refugees, and 20 to 40,000 women and girls were raped. The world learned the concept of 'ethnic cleansing'.**

*see also Map 10*

President Josip Broz Tito ruled federal Yugoslavia from 1944 until his death in 1980. Yugoslavia became inherently unstable. Power, except for the military, was divided between its six republics: Bosnia-Herzegovina, Croatia, Macedonia, Montenegro, Serbia and Slovenia. The presidency rotated annually between these and two provinces of Serbia, Kosovo and Vojvodina. The north was more prosperous than the south, economic inequality roughly coinciding with ethnic division. In 1989 annual inflation reached 10,000 percent. Even so, Yugoslavia might have avoided war, ethnic cleansing and concentration camps, but for the political ambitions of leaders intent on hanging on to power and avoiding democracy.

Yugoslavia 1919-91

The disintegration began in 1981 in Kosovo, a province of Serbia with a large majority of Albanians. In the 1960s, Albanian nationalists had demanded that Kosovo be made a republic and given equal status with Serbia. As a compromise in 1974, Kosovo acquired its own provincial parliament but stayed part of Serbia. In 1981, demonstrations renewed demands for a Kosovo republic and turned violent. At least nine people were killed, hundreds wounded, and 2,000 Albanians were arrested.

Serbian communist leader Slobodan Milosevic was the first major politician to play the nationalist card, by supporting the Serb minority in Kosovo, which allegedly faced severe discrimination. In March 1989, amid violent clashes, he forced the Kosovo parliament to surrender the province's autonomy. As Milosevic continued to press Serbia's interests against the rest of the federation, Slovenian communist leader Milan Kucan took defensive action. He became a nationalist leader by default. In Croatia, Franjo Tudjman, nationalist dissident and former Communist general, was elected President. Slovenia and Croatia declared independence in June 1991, Macedonia five months later and Bosnia-Herzegovina in 1992.

In a ten day war, Slovenia successfully resisted the Yugoslav army's attempt to smother its independence. The army's officer corps was predominantly Serb and armed Serb nationalists in Croatia and Bosnia-Herzegovina. Croatia maintained its independence despite losing territory in the war from July to December 1991.

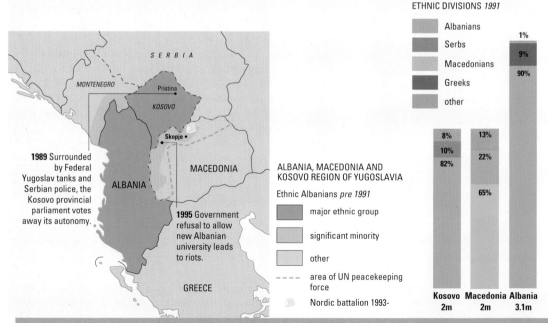

**1989** Surrounded by Federal Yugoslav tanks and Serbian police, the Kosovo provincial parliament votes away its autonomy.

**1995** Government refusal to allow new Albanian university leads to riots.

ALBANIA, MACEDONIA AND KOSOVO REGION OF YUGOSLAVIA

Ethnic Albanians *pre 1991*

- major ethnic group
- significant minority
- other
- - - - area of UN peacekeeping force
- Nordic battalion 1993-

ETHNIC DIVISIONS *1991*

- Albanians
- Serbs
- Macedonians
- Greeks
- other

| | Kosovo 2m | Macedonia 2m | Albania 3.1m |
|---|---|---|---|
| | 82% | 65% | 90% |
| | 10% | 22% | 9% |
| | 8% | 13% | 1% |

The war in Bosnia-Herzegovina began in April 1992. The Serb aim was to form Greater Serbia. The strategy was to take territory and clear it of non-Serbs. The tactic was terror.

UN forces arrived in Croatia and Bosnia in 1992. After several changes of mandate, their role was to provide humanitarian aid, peacekeeping and protecting six 'safe areas'. But there was no peace to keep in Bosnia, the forces were too small to provide protection, and aid was intermittent.

In 1993, Croats and Muslims fought an intense civil war in central Bosnia. The formation of a Muslim-Croat Federation in March 1994 did not end disputes and tensions.

In spring 1995, to deter threatened US bombing raids, Serb forces took UN soldiers hostage. They swept on to occupy the 'safe areas' of Srebrenica and Zepa, massacring several thousand Muslims. Two months later the USA stepped in. Croatian and Bosnian military successes were the background to the Dayton Peace Agreement in November 1995. The war stopped but neither the Bosnian government nor the Bosnian Serbs were satisfied. Bosnia-Herzegovina was formally united but in fact divided.

The Dayton Agreement did not consider Kosovo. Albanians quietly declared Kosovo an independent republic and elected a national parliament but the Serb authorities do not recognize it. Tens of thousands of Albanians have lost their jobs and many have been intimidated into leaving the province. Walls have been built through schools to divide Albanian and Serb children.

An escalation of conflict in Kosovo would mean refugees flooding into Albania and Macedonia. Neither state would be well equipped to deal with them. Albania is poor and has not recovered from a violent transition from dictatorship to uncertain democracy in 1991. After declaring independence, Macedonia, though helped by a UN Nordic battalion with US back up, faced four years of isolation and sanctions. Greece did not accept the new republic's right to its name and waged a diplomatic and economic campaign against it. An agreement of 1995 allows Macedonia to use its own name, but may be unique in world history as an agreement between two parties in which neither one is named.

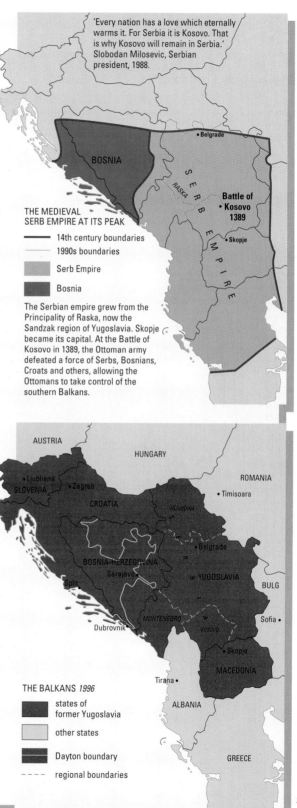

'Every nation has a love which eternally warms it. For Serbia it is Kosovo. That is why Kosovo will remain in Serbia.'
Slobodan Milosevic, Serbian president, 1988.

**THE MEDIEVAL SERB EMPIRE AT ITS PEAK**

— 14th century boundaries
— 1990s boundaries
▨ Serb Empire
▨ Bosnia

The Serbian empire grew from the Principality of Raska, now the Sandzak region of Yugoslavia. Skopje became its capital. At the Battle of Kosovo in 1389, the Ottoman army defeated a force of Serbs, Bosnians, Croats and others, allowing the Ottomans to take control of the southern Balkans.

**THE BALKANS** *1996*
▨ states of former Yugoslavia
▨ other states
▨ Dayton boundary
- - - - regional boundaries

# 10 ETHNIC CLEANSING

Ethnic cleansing has been ruthless and effective. People from different ethnic groups who used to live together in Bosnia-Herzegovina and Croatia have now moved apart.

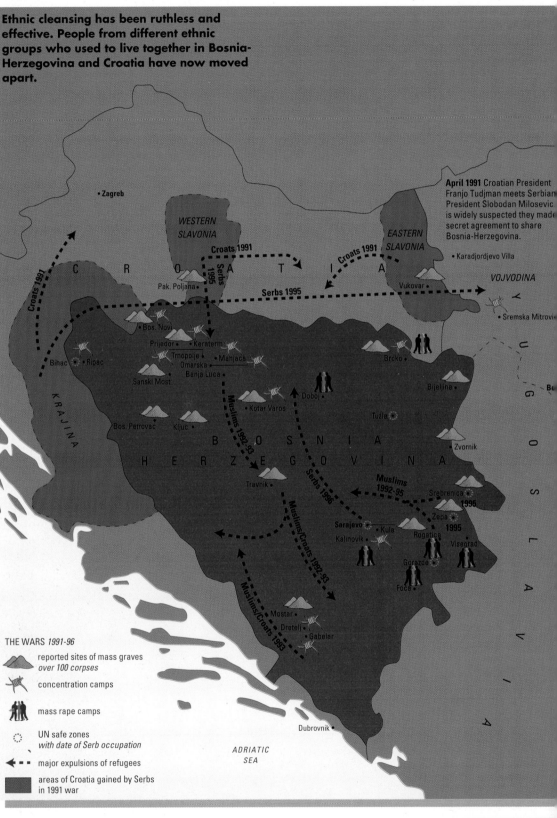

**April 1991** Croatian President Franjo Tudjman meets Serbian President Slobodan Milosevic is widely suspected they made secret agreement to share Bosnia-Herzegovina.

THE WARS *1991-96*

- reported sites of mass graves *over 100 corpses*
- concentration camps
- mass rape camps
- UN safe zones *with date of Serb occupation*
- major expulsions of refugees
- areas of Croatia gained by Serbs in 1991 war

Map labels: Zagreb, WESTERN SLAVONIA, Croats 1991, Croats 1991, EASTERN SLAVONIA, Karadjordjevo Villa, VOJVODINA, CROATIA, Serbs 1995, Pak. Poljana, Serbs 1995, Vukovar, Sremska Mitrovie, Bos. Novi, Prijedor, Keraterm, Brcko, Bijeljina, Be, Bihac, Ripac, Trnopolje, Omarska, Manjaca, Sanski Most, Banja Luca, Muslims 1992-93, Doboj, Tuzla, KRAJINA, Kotar Varos, Bos. Petrovac, Kljuc, BOSNIA, Zvornik, HERZEGOVINA, Serbs 1996, Muslims 1992-95, Srebrenica, 1995, Travnik, Zepa, 1995, Muslims/Croats 1992-93, Sarajevo, Kula, Rogatica, Visegrad, Kalinovik, Gorazde, Foca, Muslims/Croats 1993, Mostar, Dretelj, Gabelar, Y U G O S L A V I A, Dubrovnik, ADRIATIC SEA

Serb forces backed by the Yugoslav Federal Army took Krajina and parts of Slavonia from Croatia in the summer and autumn of 1991. In the first four months of war in Bosnia-Herzegovina, April to August 1992, local Serbs made major territorial gains, with the aid of arms supplied by Serb officers in the Yugoslav Federal Army. In 1993, Cyrus Vance for the UN and David Owen for the European Union brokered a peace agreement to divide Bosnia. Condemned in the USA for sanctioning 'ethnic cleansing', the agreement was rejected by the Bosnian Serbs for allowing them only 43 percent of Bosnia when they had taken as much as 70 percent by force.

In mid 1995, Croatia's offensives regained most of the territory lost to Serbs in 1991, with an army trained and equipped by the USA. In the autumn, backed by NATO air strikes, Bosnian offensives took back a third of the land taken by the Bosnian Serbs, Republika Srpska. Against this background, US diplomats negotiated the Dayton Agreement in November 1995 to divide Bosnia-Herzegovina. Though formally part of a single state, the Serb area is largely autonomous. Republika Srpska consists of 49 percent of the territory. The Muslim-Croat Federation holds 51 percent.

LIVING TOGETHER IN BOSNIA-HERZEGOVINA *pre 1991*

More than 50% of population was:

- Serb
- Croat
- Muslim
- no majority ethnic group

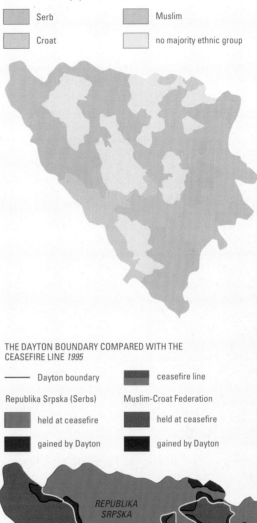

THE DAYTON BOUNDARY COMPARED WITH THE CEASEFIRE LINE *1995*

- Dayton boundary
- ceasefire line

Republika Srpska (Serbs)
- held at ceasefire
- gained by Dayton

Muslim-Croat Federation
- held at ceasefire
- gained by Dayton

REPUBLIKA SRPSKA

MUSLIM-CROAT FEDERATION

MOVING APART
Croats, Muslims and Serbs in Bosnia
*1991 (pre war) and January 1996*

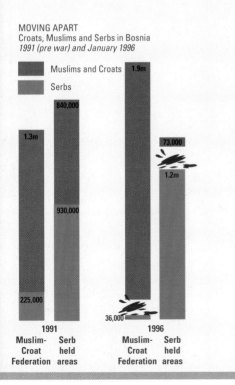

- Muslims and Croats
- Serbs

1.9m
840,000
73,000
1.3m
1.2m
930,000
225,000
36,000

1991
Muslim-Croat Federation | Serb held areas

1996
Muslim-Croat Federation | Serb held areas

# 11 EDGE OF EMPIRE

**The break up of the Soviet Union ignited several conflicts in the Caucasus. Russia imposed a fragile peace in some areas even while its forces were bombarding towns and villages in Chechnya.**

The Caucasus is home to 28 ethnic groups numbering 5,000 people or more. They differ from each other by combinations of language, religion, history, homeland and culture. Mongol, Persian, Ottoman and Russian empires fought over their lands for centuries. Much of the history is bitter. The Ottoman empire killed or starved to death one and a half million Armenians between 1895 and 1920. In February 1944, Soviet security forces rounded up the entire Chechen nation of 400,000, the whole Ingush nation of almost 100,000, and 100,000 others from the north Caucasus, and deported them to Central Asia. They were not allowed to return until 1957.

At the end of the 1980s, greater openness in the USSR encouraged democrats to demand national independence. Their momentum became irresistible and the USSR broke up in 1991. In the ethnic patchwork of the Caucasus, the independence of one ethnic group was to threaten another with subjugation. The impulse towards independence and national rights slipped easily into aggressive chauvinism. Democracy was fragile, economic decline was sharp and political order collapsed. In Georgia, power belonged to the warlords as the country was torn by three civil wars. Armenian and Karabakh forces occupied part of Azerbaijan. Within Russia, a faction in Chechnya saw a chance for seizing national independence. North Ossetian militias drove 60,000 Ingush from their homes.

Russia attempted to reassert itself in the region. It imposed ceasefires in Georgia but was unable to resolve conflicts either there, or between Armenia and Azerbaijan. In Chechnya, what was meant to be a swift campaign to crush Chechen independence in late 1994 became a prolonged war.

**1991 USSR**

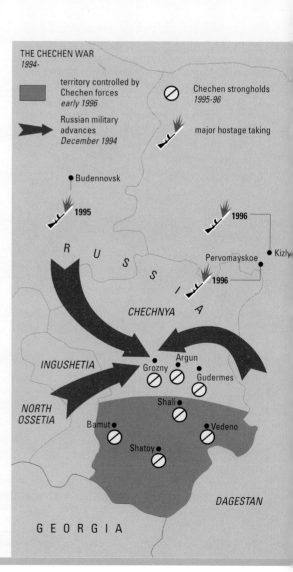

THE CHECHEN WAR
*1994-*

territory controlled by Chechen forces *early 1996*

Russian military advances *December 1994*

Chechen strongholds *1995-96*

major hostage taking

Novorossiisk

Gud

Budennovsk

1995

1996

R U S S I A

Pervomayskoe • Kizly

1996

CHECHNYA

INGUSHETIA

Grozny  Argun

Gudermes

NORTH OSSETIA

Bamut •    Shali •

Vedeno •

Shatoy •

DAGESTAN

GEORGIA

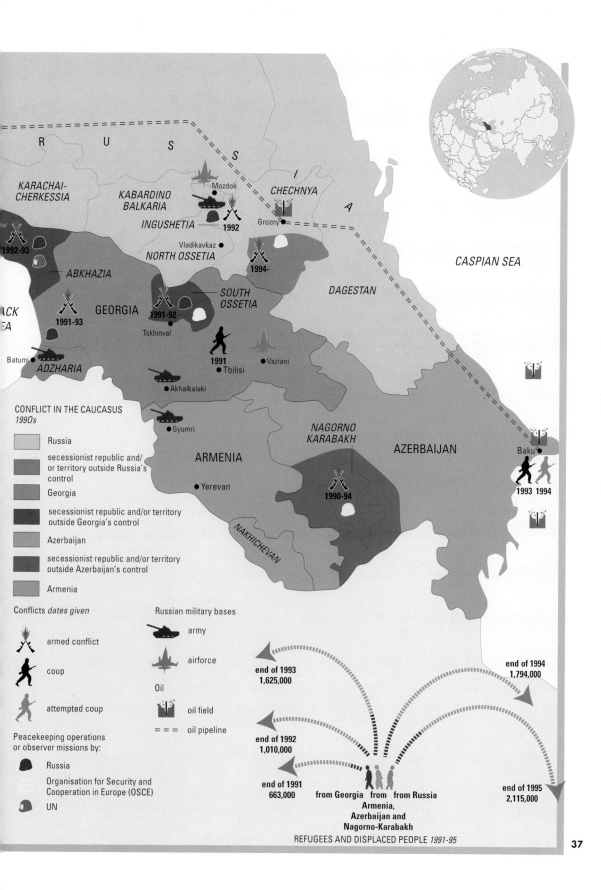

R   U   S   S   I   A

KARACHAI-
CHERKESSIA

KABARDINO
BALKARIA

INGUSHETIA

**1992**

CHECHNYA

Mozdok

Grozny

**1992-93**

ABKHAZIA

Vladikavkaz

NORTH OSSETIA

**1994-**

CASPIAN SEA

GEORGIA

SOUTH
OSSETIA

DAGESTAN

**1991-93**

**1991-92**

Tskhinval

BLACK
SEA

Batumi

ADZHARIA

**1991**

Tbilisi

Vaziani

Akhalkalaki

CONFLICT IN THE CAUCASUS
*1990s*

Gyumri

NAGORNO
KARABAKH

AZERBAIJAN

Baku

ARMENIA

**1993 1994**

|   | Russia |
|---|---|
|   | secessionist republic and/<br>or territory outside Russia's<br>control |
|   | Georgia |
|   | secessionist republic and/or territory<br>outside Georgia's control |
|   | Azerbaijan |
|   | secessionist republic and/or territory<br>outside Azerbaijan's control |
|   | Armenia |

Yerevan

**1990-94**

NAKHICHEVAN

Conflicts *dates given*

Russian military bases

army

armed conflict

airforce

coup

Oil

oil field

attempted coup

=== oil pipeline

Peacekeeping operations
or observer missions by:

Russia

Organisation for Security and
Cooperation in Europe (OSCE)

UN

end of 1993
1,625,000

end of 1994
1,794,000

end of 1992
1,010,000

end of 1991
663,000

from Georgia   from   from Russia
Armenia,
Azerbaijan and
Nagorno-Karabakh

end of 1995
2,115,000

REFUGEES AND DISPLACED PEOPLE *1991-95*

Dan Smith *The State of War and Peace Atlas* 3rd edition Copyright © Myriad Editions Limited

# 12 FROM WAR TO WAR

**War has become a pattern of life in the highlands and deserts of Afghanistan and Tajikistan. Ethnic, sub ethnic and clan armies are engaged in endless fighting. Large parts of both countries now have no effective government.**

In April 1978, King Daoud of Afghanistan was deposed by a Communist coup. The new regime's main political strength lay in the capital. Elsewhere an essentially feudal society resisted all political change, especially land reform. The USSR gave Kabul financial, military and technical assistance, but the opposition only grew stronger.

In December 1979 Soviet forces moved in, to install a new group of leaders. They faced massive armed resistance from the *mujahideen* guerrillas, supported by Iran, Pakistan, Saudi Arabia and the USA. The USA alone is estimated to have provided over a million rifles to the guerrillas during the 1980s, along with many other kinds of weapons.

For the USSR, the costly and hopeless war in Afghanistan contributed to public distrust in the Soviet leadership and growing social erosion. By February 1989 all Soviet forces were withdrawn from Afghanistan. But the Kabul government survived for three more years. By the time it fell, the long war had sown distrust and rivalry among the *mujahideen* leaders. In less than a year they turned their forces on each other.

The breakup of the USSR at the end of 1991 led to a power struggle in Tajikistan that is now fought out between ethnic factions. Heavy fighting created large numbers of refugees, some of whom fled to Afghanistan where they made links with ethnic Tajik forces. Out of this came support in the form of finance and training; in return Tajiks in Tajikistan fight alongside their kin from Afghanistan. Negotiations have achieved several ceasefires and may have prevented worse fighting but have not brought peace.

In 1995 a new force emerged in Afghanistan - the Taliban troops, religious students proclaiming the goal of Islamic rule, mostly Pushtuns, aided by Pakistan. Though the number of refugees declined as the 1990s went on, resources provided by the international community for relief in this enormous human disaster diminished much faster.

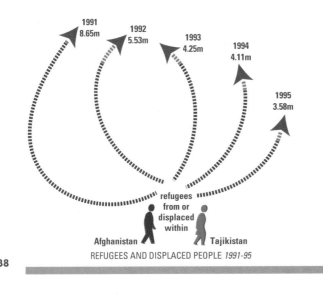

REFUGEES AND DISPLACED PEOPLE *1991-95*

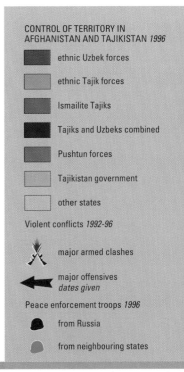

CONTROL OF TERRITORY IN
AFGHANISTAN AND TAJIKISTAN *1996*

- ethnic Uzbek forces
- ethnic Tajik forces
- Ismailite Tajiks
- Tajiks and Uzbeks combined
- Pushtun forces
- Tajikistan government
- other states

Violent conflicts *1992-96*

- major armed clashes
- major offensives *dates given*

Peace enforcement troops *1996*

- from Russia
- from neighbouring states

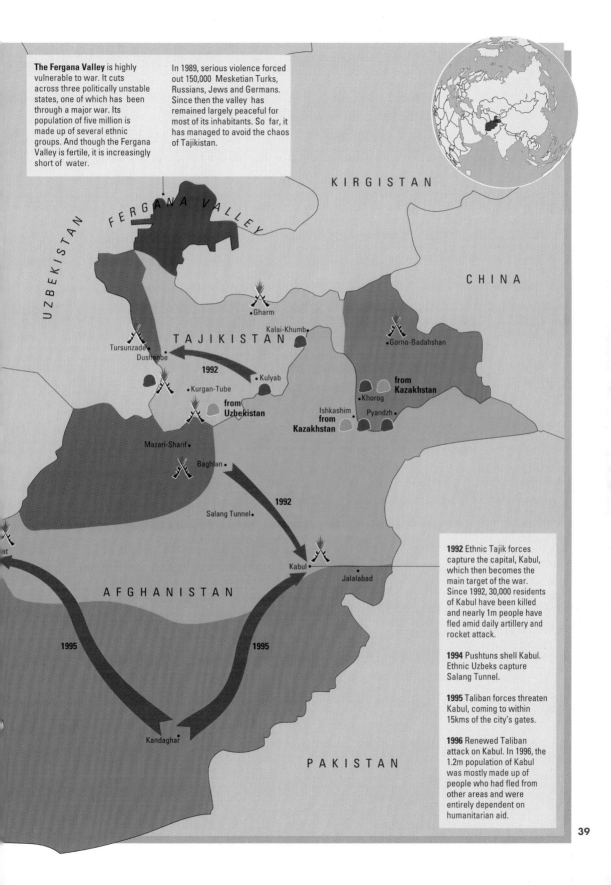

**The Fergana Valley** is highly vulnerable to war. It cuts across three politically unstable states, one of which has been through a major war. Its population of five million is made up of several ethnic groups. And though the Fergana Valley is fertile, it is increasingly short of water.

In 1989, serious violence forced out 150,000 Mesketian Turks, Russians, Jews and Germans. Since then the valley has remained largely peaceful for most of its inhabitants. So far, it has managed to avoid the chaos of Tajikistan.

KIRGISTAN

CHINA

UZBEKISTAN

FERGANA VALLEY

•Gharm

Kalai-Khumb•

TAJIKISTAN

•Gorno-Badahshan

Tursunzade•
Dushanbe•

1992

•Kulyab

**from Kazakhstan**

•Kurgan-Tube

**from Uzbekistan**

•Khorog

Ishkashim
**from Kazakhstan**

Pyandzh•

Mazari-Sharif•

Baghlan •

1992

Salang Tunnel•

at

Kabul •

Jalalabad•

AFGHANISTAN

1995

1995

Kandaghar•

PAKISTAN

**1992** Ethnic Tajik forces capture the capital, Kabul, which then becomes the main target of the war. Since 1992, 30,000 residents of Kabul have been killed and nearly 1m people have fled amid daily artillery and rocket attack.

**1994** Pushtuns shell Kabul. Ethnic Uzbeks capture Salang Tunnel.

**1995** Taliban forces threaten Kabul, coming to within 15kms of the city's gates.

**1996** Renewed Taliban attack on Kabul. In 1996, the 1.2m population of Kabul was mostly made up of people who had fled from other areas and were entirely dependent on humanitarian aid.

# 13 NATIONLESS NATION

Dan Smith *The State of War and Peace Atlas* 3rd edition Copyright © Myriad Editions Limited

**The Kurdish people are united by geography, history and by their name. Everything else divides them. They have never had a unified state. Approximately one Kurd in eight is a refugee or a displaced person.**

For centuries, the people who lived in the mountains of Kurdistan were beyond the reach of the empires that sought to rule them. From this isolation grew a common sense of Kurdish identity.

The last real chance for an autonomous Kurdistan came after the First World War. The 1920 Treaty of Sèvres provided for a Kurdish nation state as part of the package that divided territories between the victorious western powers and the defeated Ottoman empire. However, Turkey's new leader, Mustafa Kemal, refused to give up any land to the Kurds though they had helped him to power. Britain and France, satisfied with their own territorial gains and wary of disturbing a fragile postwar peace, were reluctant to force Kemal to back down. In 1923 a new treaty was agreed. United Kurdistan was lost.

Since then, Kurdish movements have often fought each other as fiercely as they have fought for Kurdish independence. In Iraq, every Kurdish uprising from the 1920s until the 1980s met armed opposition from rival Kurdish factions as well as from government forces. During the 1990s, while Iraqi Kurds were under attack from Saddam Hussein's government in Baghdad, the Kurdistan Democratic Party (KDP) and the Patriotic Union of Kurdistan (PUK) remained locked in combat. The KDP has also fought against the Turkish Kurdistan Worker's Party (PKK) even aiding Turkish government offensives against the PKK.

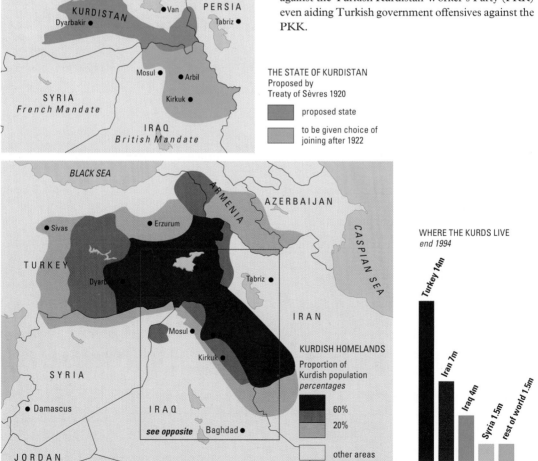

**1920**

OTTOMAN TURKEY

• Sivas          • Erzurum

KURDISTAN          • Van          PERSIA
Dyarbakir •                        Tabriz •

Mosul •   • Arbil

SYRIA
*French Mandate*          Kirkuk •

IRAQ
*British Mandate*

**THE STATE OF KURDISTAN**
Proposed by
Treaty of Sèvres 1920

■ proposed state

■ to be given choice of joining after 1922

BLACK SEA

• Sivas          • Erzurum          ARMENIA          AZERBAIJAN

TURKEY

Dyarb          Tabriz •          CASPIAN SEA

Mosul •

Kirkuk •          IRAN

SYRIA

• Damascus          IRAQ

*see opposite*   Baghdad •

JORDAN

**KURDISH HOMELANDS**
Proportion of
Kurdish population
*percentages*

■ 60%
■ 20%
□ other areas

**WHERE THE KURDS LIVE**
*end 1994*

Turkey 14m
Iran 7m
Iraq 4m
Syria 1.5m
rest of world 1.5m

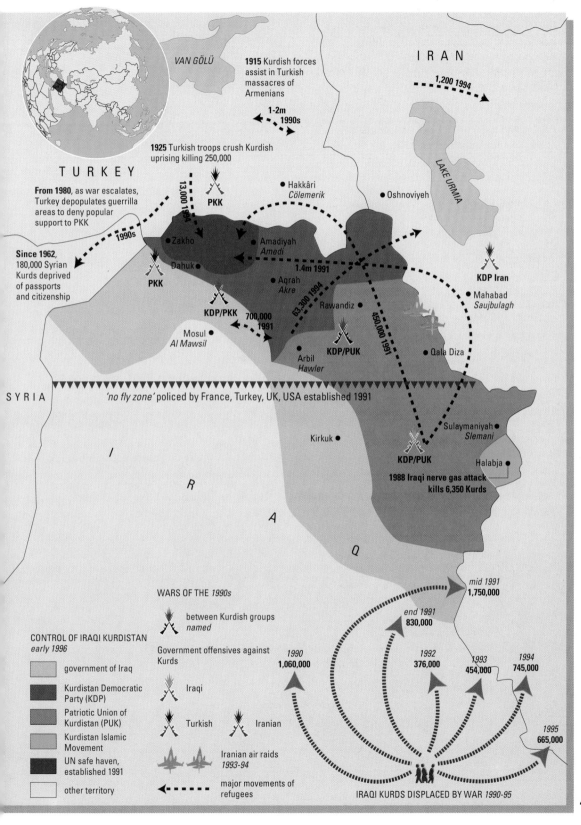

VAN GÖLÜ

IRAN

**1915** Kurdish forces assist in Turkish massacres of Armenians

1,200 1994

1-2m 1990s

LAKE URMIA

TURKEY

**1925** Turkish troops crush Kurdish uprising killing 250,000

**From 1980**, as war escalates, Turkey depopulates guerrilla areas to deny popular support to PKK

13,000 1994

PKK

● Hakkâri
*Cölemerik*

● Oshnoviyeh

1990s

● Zakho

Dahuk ●

PKK

**Since 1962**, 180,000 Syrian Kurds deprived of passports and citizenship

● Amadiyah
*Amedi*

● Aqrah
*Akre*

1.4m 1991

63,300 1994

KDP/PKK

700,000 1991

Rawandiz ●

KDP Iran

● Mahabad
*Saujbulagh*

450,000 1991

Mosul ●
*Al Mawsil*

Arbil ●
*Hawler*

KDP/PUK

● Qala Diza

SYRIA

▼▼▼▼▼▼▼▼▼▼▼▼▼▼▼▼▼▼▼▼▼▼▼▼▼▼▼▼▼▼

*'no fly zone'* policed by France, Turkey, UK, USA established 1991

I

Kirkuk ●

R

A

Sulaymaniyah ●
*Slemani*

KDP/PUK

Halabja ●

**1988 Iraqi nerve gas attack kills 6,350 Kurds**

Q

mid 1991
**1,750,000**

WARS OF THE *1990s*

🔫 between Kurdish groups
named

end 1991
**830,000**

CONTROL OF IRAQI KURDISTAN
*early 1996*

Government offensives against Kurds

*1990*
**1,060,000**

*1992*
**376,000**

*1993*
**454,000**

*1994*
**745,000**

government of Iraq

🔫 Iraqi

Kurdistan Democratic Party (KDP)

Patriotic Union of Kurdistan (PUK)

🔫 Turkish     🔫 Iranian

*1995*
**665,000**

Kurdistan Islamic Movement

✈✈ Iranian air raids
*1993-94*

UN safe haven, established 1991

other territory

← - - major movements of refugees

IRAQI KURDS DISPLACED BY WAR *1990-95*

**41**

# 14 HOLY LANDS

**Israel has been permanently at war since its foundation half a century ago. Peace agreements with the Palestine Liberation Organization are altering the conflict but not ending it.**

Israel and Palestine together contain places of deep significance for three major religions: Christianity, Islam and Judaism. For nine centuries, since the first crusade in 1095, faith has been a focus for conflict.

The region was part of the Ottoman Empire from the early 1500s until the end of the First World War when Britain took control. By then the Zionist movement was underway, aiming to make Israel the homeland for all Jews. On the eve of the Second World War, Britain tentatively agreed to establish separate Jewish and Arab states – the 'partition plan'.

The mass murder of Jews during the war years made the State of Israel inevitable. The UN proposed a partition plan in 1947. Israel was founded in 1948 and extended its territory beyond the UN plan. It expanded again in 1967, and in the early 1980s took control of a 'security zone' in southern Lebanon. In 1948, Arabs were two thirds of the population in the area that is now Israel and the Occupied Territories; in 1995, they were one third. Millions went into exile. In 1995 there were still over four million Palestinian refugees.

Peace agreements in 1993 and 1995 between Israel and the Palestine Liberation Organization assigned some local government powers to a new Palestine Authority. The peace process inflamed activists on each side. Armed Islamist opposition groups, Hamas and Islamic Jihad, took up the fight against Israel supported by the Hezbollah organization from Lebanon. The depths of opposition to the peace process among some Israelis was shown by the assassination of Prime Minister Yitzhak Rabin in 1995. In the first two years of 'peace', 403 people were killed by military action. In 1996 there was a new escalation of conflict in Southern Lebanon, forcing 400,000 people from their homes.

The issues have not changed. For Arabs in both Israel and the Occupied Territories, the conflict is about the denial of rights and freedoms, full citizenship and a sense of belonging. For Israel, it is about the very right to exist.

Behind politics lie land and water. The River Jordan is sluggish where it once flowed freely. Keeping Israel's desert green demands substantial supplies from underground water resources — the West Bank aquifers. Palestinians have been banned from sinking new wells since Israel took control in 1967.

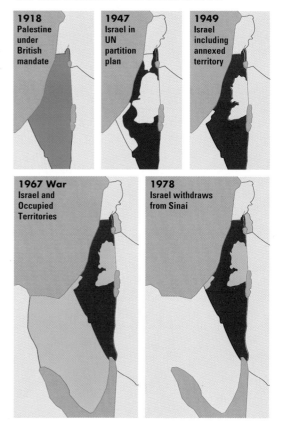

**1918** Palestine under British mandate

**1947** Israel in UN partition plan

**1949** Israel including annexed territory

**1967 War** Israel and Occupied Territories

**1978** Israel withdraws from Sinai

water allocated to 130,000 Jewish settlers from West Bank aquifers *1994*
30m metres$^3$
230 metres$^3$ each

water allocated to 1.4m Palestinians from West Bank aquifers *1994*
115m metres$^3$
82 metres$^3$ each

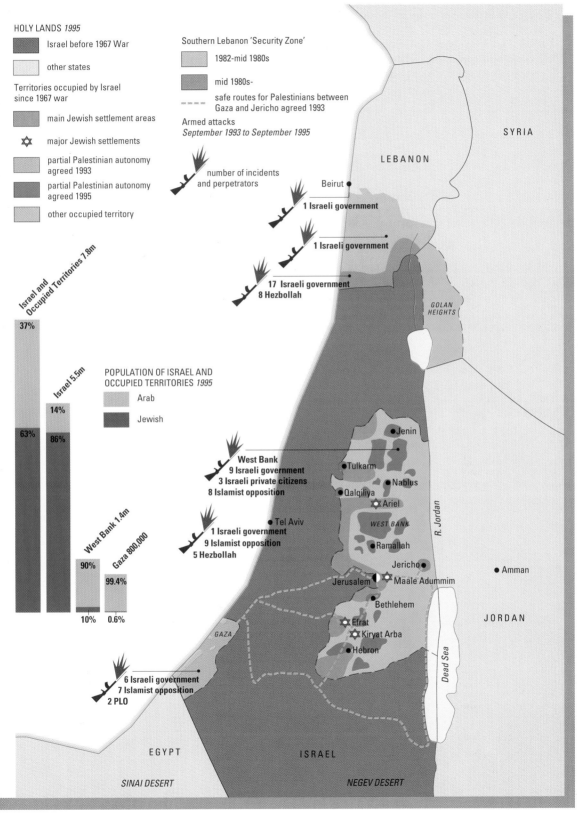

HOLY LANDS *1995*

Israel before 1967 War

other states

Territories occupied by Israel
since 1967 war

main Jewish settlement areas

✡ major Jewish settlements

partial Palestinian autonomy
agreed 1993

partial Palestinian autonomy
agreed 1995

other occupied territory

Southern Lebanon 'Security Zone'

1982-mid 1980s

mid 1980s-

- - - safe routes for Palestinians between
Gaza and Jericho agreed 1993

Armed attacks
*September 1993 to September 1995*

number of incidents
and perpetrators

Israel and
Occupied Territories 7.8m

37%

63%

Israel 5.5m

14%

86%

POPULATION OF ISRAEL AND
OCCUPIED TERRITORIES *1995*

Arab

Jewish

West Bank 1.4m

90%

10%

Gaza 800,000

99.4%

0.6%

SYRIA

LEBANON

Beirut ●

1 Israeli government

1 Israeli government

17 Israeli government
8 Hezbollah

GOLAN
HEIGHTS

●Jenin

West Bank
9 Israeli government
3 Israeli private citizens
8 Islamist opposition

●Tulkarm

●Nablus

●Qalqiliya

✡Ariel

● Tel Aviv

*WEST BANK*

R. Jordan

1 Israeli government
9 Islamist opposition
5 Hezbollah

●Ramallah

Jericho ●

● Amman

Jerusalem ● ✡ Maale Adummim

Bethlehem ●

JORDAN

✡ Efrat

*GAZA*

✡ Kiryat Arba

6 Israeli government
7 Islamist opposition
2 PLO

● Hebron

Dead Sea

EGYPT

ISRAEL

SINAI DESERT

NEGEV DESERT

43

# 15 MILITANT FAITH

Islamist movements are growing in response to increasing distrust of political elites and resentment at the growing gap between rich and poor. The movements vary in their objectives, tactics and doctrines. They all demand a break with Western secular ways.

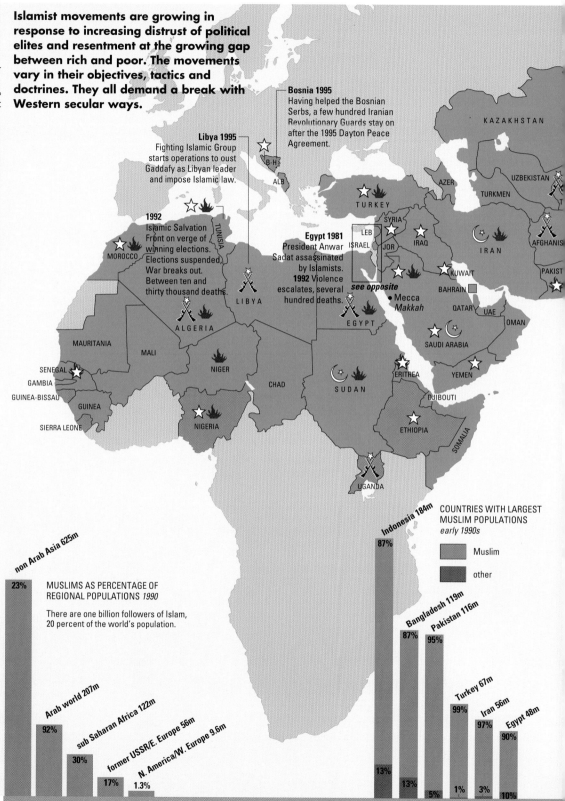

Dan Smith *The State of War and Peace Atlas* 3rd edition Copyright © Myriad Editions Limited

**Bosnia 1995**
Having helped the Bosnian Serbs, a few hundred Iranian Revolutionary Guards stay on after the 1995 Dayton Peace Agreement.

**Libya 1995**
Fighting Islamic Group starts operations to oust Gaddafy as Libyan leader and impose Islamic law.

**1992**
Islamic Salvation Front on verge of winning elections. Elections suspended. War breaks out. Between ten and thirty thousand deaths.

**Egypt 1981**
President Anwar Sadat assassinated by Islamists.
**1992** Violence escalates, several hundred deaths.

*see opposite*

KAZAKHSTAN

B-H
ALB
AZER
UZBEKISTAN
TURKMEN
TURKEY
SYRIA
LEB
ISRAEL
JOR
IRAQ
IRAN
AFGHANIS
PAKIST
KUWAIT
BAHRAIN
Mecca
Makkah
QATAR
UAE
OMAN
TUNISIA
MOROCCO
LIBYA
EGYPT
SAUDI ARABIA
YEMEN
ALGERIA
MAURITANIA
MALI
NIGER
CHAD
SUDAN
ERITREA
DJIBOUTI
SENEGAL
GAMBIA
GUINEA-BISSAU
GUINEA
SIERRA LEONE
NIGERIA
ETHIOPIA
SOMALIA
UGANDA

## COUNTRIES WITH LARGEST MUSLIM POPULATIONS
*early 1990s*

Muslim
other

## MUSLIMS AS PERCENTAGE OF REGIONAL POPULATIONS *1990*

There are one billion followers of Islam, 20 percent of the world's population.

non Arab Asia 625m — 23%
Arab world 207m — 92%
sub Saharan Africa 122m — 30%
former USSR/E. Europe 56m — 17%
N. America/W. Europe 9.6m — 1.3%

Indonesia 184m — 87% / 13%
Bangladesh 119m — 87% / 13%
Pakistan 116m — 95% / 5%
Turkey 67m — 99% / 1%
Iran 56m — 97% / 3%
Egypt 48m — 90% / 10%

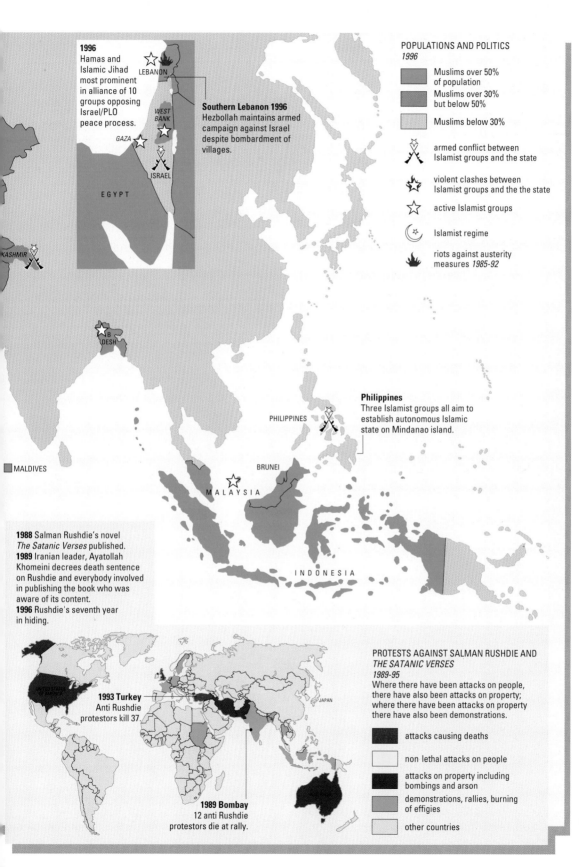

**1996**
Hamas and Islamic Jihad most prominent in alliance of 10 groups opposing Israel/PLO peace process.

LEBANON

WEST BANK

GAZA

ISRAEL

EGYPT

**Southern Lebanon 1996**
Hezbollah maintains armed campaign against Israel despite bombardment of villages.

POPULATIONS AND POLITICS
*1996*

Muslims over 50% of population

Muslims over 30% but below 50%

Muslims below 30%

armed conflict between Islamist groups and the state

violent clashes between Islamist groups and the the state

active Islamist groups

Islamist regime

riots against austerity measures *1985-92*

KASHMIR

B DESH

MALDIVES

PHILIPPINES

**Philippines**
Three Islamist groups all aim to establish autonomous Islamic state on Mindanao island.

BRUNEI

MALAYSIA

INDONESIA

**1988** Salman Rushdie's novel *The Satanic Verses* published.
**1989** Iranian leader, Ayatollah Khomeini decrees death sentence on Rushdie and everybody involved in publishing the book who was aware of its content.
**1996** Rushdie's seventh year in hiding.

UNITED STATES OF AMERICA

JAPAN

**1993 Turkey**
Anti Rushdie protestors kill 37.

**1989 Bombay**
12 anti Rushdie protestors die at rally.

PROTESTS AGAINST SALMAN RUSHDIE AND *THE SATANIC VERSES*
*1989-95*
Where there have been attacks on people, there have also been attacks on property; where there have been attacks on property there have also been demonstrations.

attacks causing deaths

non lethal attacks on people

attacks on property including bombings and arson

demonstrations, rallies, burning of effigies

other countries

45

# 16 AFTER THE RAJ

**The Indian subcontinent knew no peace under the British empire. It has known no peace since independence.**

For 2,000 years power in India was split between a great diversity of states and statelets. Imperial conquest brought unity of a kind, first with the Moguls in the seventeenth century, then with the British Raj from about 1820. It remained a region of many languages and three major religions.

Independence, in 1947, was deeply divisive. While Gandhi and the nationalists dreamed of unity, other political leaders preferred to emphasize what divides people, not what unites them. Where once different religions co-existed, there was a violent partition of largely Hindu India from mostly Muslim Pakistan.

In 1972, Pakistan split with equal violence and East Pakistan became the state of Bangladesh. Burma has not known one day of peace since independence, and Sri Lanka, since 1977, has known but few.

India has been riven by civil wars, some of them fought for regional independence. Renewed religious conflict in the 1990s focussed on the destruction of the Ayodhya Mosque which allegedly stood on a Hindu shrine.

India and Pakistan have fought three wars, the last in 1971. The confrontation continues. India accuses Pakistan of fomenting war in Kashmir. Both states have nuclear weapons. India carried out a nuclear test in 1974; Pakistan had nuclear capability by 1990. In May 1990, Pakistan's forces were put on alert in response to Indian army manoeuvres near the border. Both sides made their nuclear weapons ready. The CIA called it 'the most dangerous nuclear situation we have ever faced' and 'far more frightening than the Cuban missile crisis' in 1962.

Dan Smith *The State of War and Peace Atlas* 3rd edition Copyright © Myriad Editions Limited

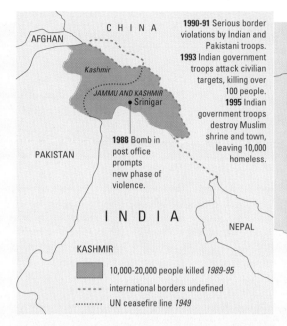

**1990-91** Serious border violations by Indian and Pakistani troops.
**1993** Indian government troops attack civilian targets, killing over 100 people.
**1995** Indian government troops destroy Muslim shrine and town, leaving 10,000 homeless.

**1988** Bomb in post office prompts new phase of violence.

KASHMIR

10,000-20,000 people killed *1989-95*

- - - - international borders undefined

.......... UN ceasefire line *1949*

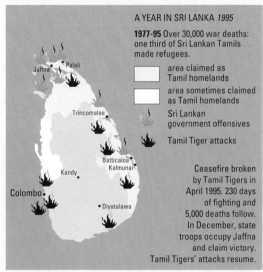

**A YEAR IN SRI LANKA** *1995*

**1977-95** Over 30,000 war deaths: one third of Sri Lankan Tamils made refugees.

area claimed as Tamil homelands

area sometimes claimed as Tamil homelands

Sri Lankan government offensives

Tamil Tiger attacks

Ceasefire broken by Tamil Tigers in April 1995. 230 days of fighting and 5,000 deaths follow. In December, state troops occupy Jaffna and claim victory. Tamil Tigers' attacks resume.

## 1920s The British Raj

In 1919, British forces in Amritsar opened fire on a human rights rally of 10,000 people killing 379 and wounding 1,200. An army enquiry concluded this was a 'an error of judgement'.

## 1947-48 Partition

Partition of India and Pakistan led to war and the flight of about 14 million refugees: over 5.3 million Hindus and 8.6 million Muslims. One million perished.

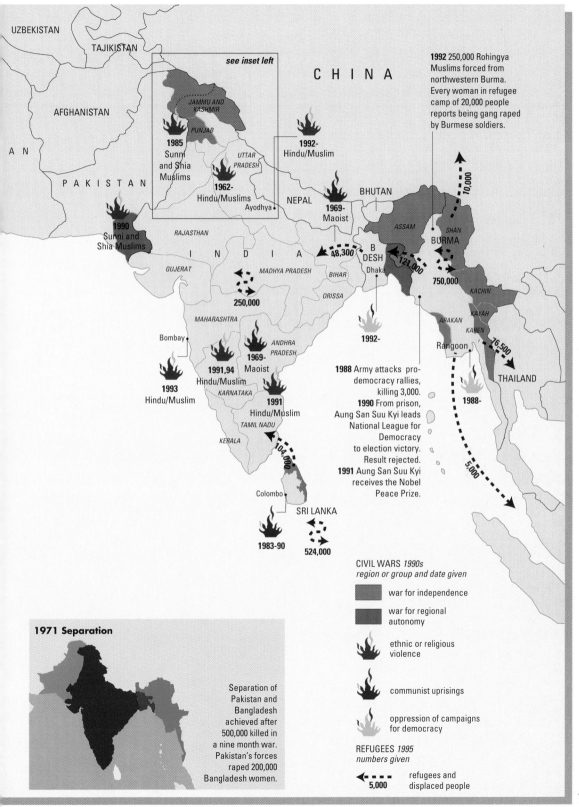

UZBEKISTAN

TAJIKISTAN

AFGHANISTAN

AN

PAKISTAN

CHINA

*see inset left*

JAMMU AND KASHMIR

PUNJAB

**1985**
Sunni
and Shia
Muslims

UTTAR PRADESH

**1962-**
Hindu/Muslims
Ayodhya

**1992-**
Hindu/Muslim

NEPAL

BHUTAN

**1969-**
Maoist

RAJASTHAN

**1990**
Sunni and
Shia Muslims

GUJERAT

I N D I A

MADHYA PRADESH

BIHAR

ORISSA

48,300

B DESH
Dhaka

121,000

ASSAM

SHAN

BURMA

KACHIN

750,000

10,000

**1992** 250,000 Rohingya
Muslims forced from
northwestern Burma.
Every woman in refugee
camp of 20,000 people
reports being gang raped
by Burmese soldiers.

250,000

MAHARASHTRA

Bombay

**1991,94**
Hindu/Muslim

KARNATAKA

**1969-**
Maoist

ANDHRA
PRADESH

**1991**
Hindu/Muslim

TAMIL NADU

**1993**
Hindu/Muslim

KERALA

104,000

Colombo

SRI LANKA

**1983-90**

524,000

**1992-**

ARAKAN

KAYAH

KAREN

Rangoon

76,500

THAILAND

**1988-**

5,000

**1988** Army attacks pro-
democracy rallies,
killing 3,000.
**1990** From prison,
Aung San Suu Kyi leads
National League for
Democracy
to election victory.
Result rejected.
**1991** Aung San Suu Kyi
receives the Nobel
Peace Prize.

CIVIL WARS *1990s*
*region or group and date given*

war for independence

war for regional
autonomy

ethnic or religious
violence

communist uprisings

oppression of campaigns
for democracy

REFUGEES *1995*
*numbers given*

5,000    refugees and
displaced people

**1971 Separation**

Separation of
Pakistan and
Bangladesh
achieved after
500,000 killed in
a nine month war.
Pakistan's forces
raped 200,000
Bangladesh women.

WAR *1990-95*

Percentage of countries experiencing war,
grouped according to the UN Human
Development Index, combining prosperity,
health and education

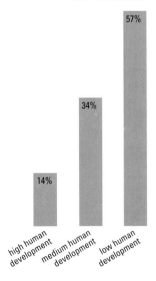

57%

34%

14%

high human
development

medium human
development

low human
development

'I meet the politicians every day. They are all frightened of each other. When I shake their hands, they are dripping with sweat. There is not one who would not murder another for the sake of an hour of political power.'

*UN Special Representative in Burundi, Ahmed Ould Abdallah, speaking in 1995*

# 17 LAND LORDS

**In Central and South America there are fewer dictators and fewer armed conflicts than there were in the 1980s. But the chief causes of conflict remain — overwhelming poverty in the cities and the dominance of a narrow elite in rural areas.**

Land is a major cause of war and violence in Central and South America. In Nicaragua, the war between the leftist Sandinistas and rightist Contras ended in 1990 but it could resume. The government has not met the demands for farmland from demobilized soldiers on both sides. Some have joined with landless peasants to attack and occupy agricultural cooperatives and state farms. Control of land also lay behind violence in Ecuador, where a 1994 land law reduced the rights of indigenous peasants. Landlords who stood to benefit from the new law organized paramilitary groups to attack protestors.

Land intertwines with other economic issues. In Chiapas in southern Mexico, the combined pressures of falling prices for farm produce, the concentration of the best quality land in the hands of the big ranch owners, and the low wages of ranchworkers fuelled an insurrection by indigenous peasants which lasted from 1994 to 1996. An influx of refugees from the war in Guatemala had caused wages to fall since the mid 1980s. When the Guatemalan refugees returned home, many found other peasants occupying their small farms. Violence followed.

Cocaine is another major cause of violence. In Colombia, security forces and paramilitary groups killed over a thousand people each year in the first half of the 1990s. Paramilitaries, backed by cattle ranchers and drug traffickers, have virtually depopulated large areas of the northwest as people flee to avoid the crossfire with the guerrillas.

In Peru, the Sendero Luminosa (Shining Path) guerrillas lost their leader and much of their territory in the first half of the 1990s. But peasants continue to suffer as both the guerrillas and the Peruvian army use terror as a routine tactic. Much of Sendero's strength is due to its profits from the drug trade. In Bolivia, the narcotics connection works differently. Police use operations ostensibly aimed at the narcotics trade as an occasion for attacking peasant leaders demanding economic justice and human rights.

GUERRILLAS *mid 1990s*

areas of major guerrilla activity

territory disputed between Ecuador and Peru
*ceded by Ecuador to Peru in 1942*

NARCOTICS AGRICULTURE
Number of hectares under cultivation

opium

coca leaf

Those who flee poverty and violence in the countryside may move on to find poverty and violence in the cities. Perhaps the worst urban violence has been in Brazil. A parliamentary commission reported that between 1987 and 1991, death squads, many consisting of off-duty police officers, killed seven thousand homeless children. The slaughter has not stopped.

In Haiti, the western hemisphere's poorest country, a US operation in 1994 restored the democratically elected President Jean-Bertrand Aristide to office, three years after a military coup had overthrown him. Though this help came only on condition that the radical Aristide would not stand for re-election, it created a chance of social and political progress.

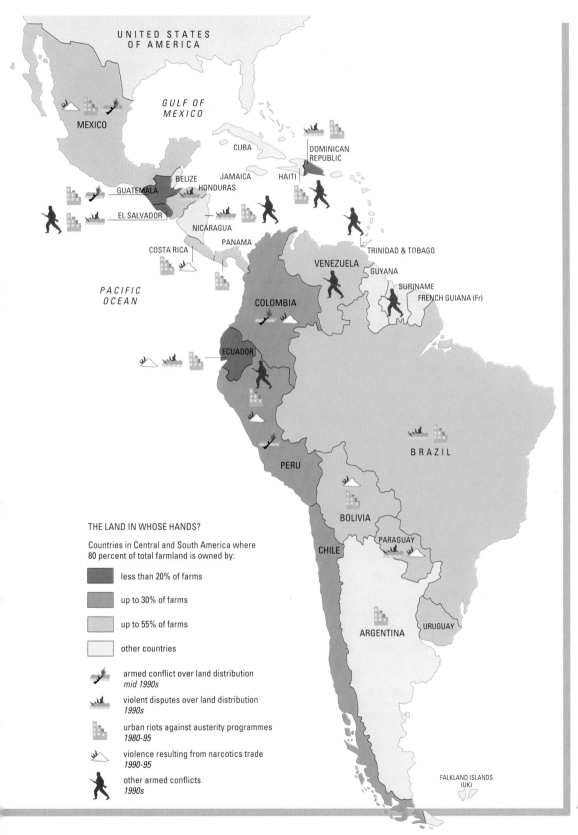

UNITED STATES
OF AMERICA

GULF OF
MEXICO

MEXICO

CUBA

DOMINICAN
REPUBLIC

JAMAICA

BELIZE
GUATEMALA
HAITI

HONDURAS

EL SALVADOR

NICARAGUA

COSTA RICA
PANAMA

TRINIDAD & TOBAGO

VENEZUELA
GUYANA

SURINAME
FRENCH GUIANA (Fr)

COLOMBIA

PACIFIC
OCEAN

ECUADOR

BRAZIL

PERU

BOLIVIA

PARAGUAY

CHILE

ARGENTINA
URUGUAY

## THE LAND IN WHOSE HANDS?

Countries in Central and South America where
80 percent of total farmland is owned by:

- less than 20% of farms
- up to 30% of farms
- up to 55% of farms
- other countries

- armed conflict over land distribution
  *mid 1990s*
- violent disputes over land distribution
  *1990s*
- urban riots against austerity programmes
  *1980-95*
- violence resulting from narcotics trade
  *1990-95*
- other armed conflicts
  *1990s*

FALKLAND ISLANDS
(UK)

# 18 THE DISPOSSESSION

In the last 20 years of the nineteenth century, Europeans conquered 85 percent of Africa in a uniquely grandiose act of theft. The continent has known little peace or prosperity since. The colonists left almost as suddenly.

Dan Smith *The State of War and Peace Atlas* 3rd edition Copyright © Myriad Editions Limited

**COLONIZER'S MAIN MOTIVE**

- strategic
- land greed
- trade, raw materials or labour
- independent state

**1857** David Livingstone, British missionary and explorer: 'I go back to Africa to try to make an open path for commerce and Christianity. Do you carry out the work which I have begun. I leave it with you!'

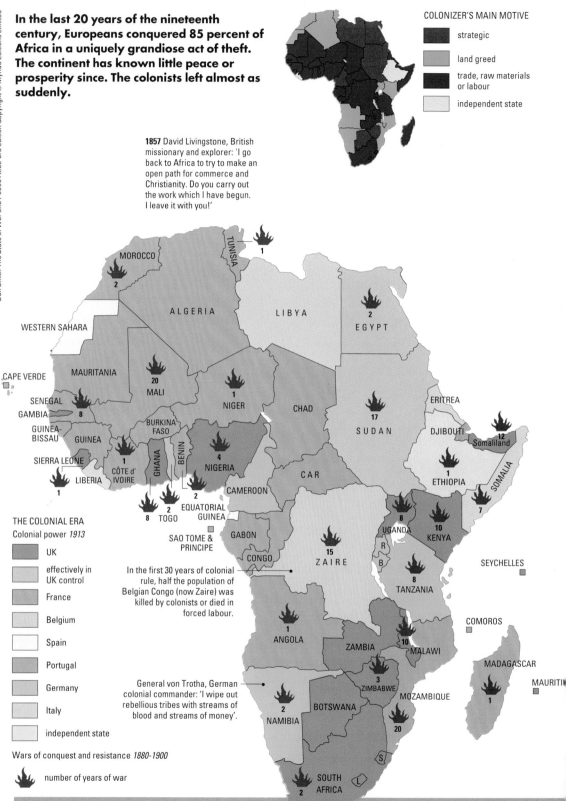

In the first 30 years of colonial rule, half the population of Belgian Congo (now Zaire) was killed by colonists or died in forced labour.

General von Trotha, German colonial commander: 'I wipe out rebellious tribes with streams of blood and streams of money'.

**THE COLONIAL ERA**
Colonial power *1913*

- UK
- effectively in UK control
- France
- Belgium
- Spain
- Portugal
- Germany
- Italy
- independent state

Wars of conquest and resistance *1880-1900*

number of years of war

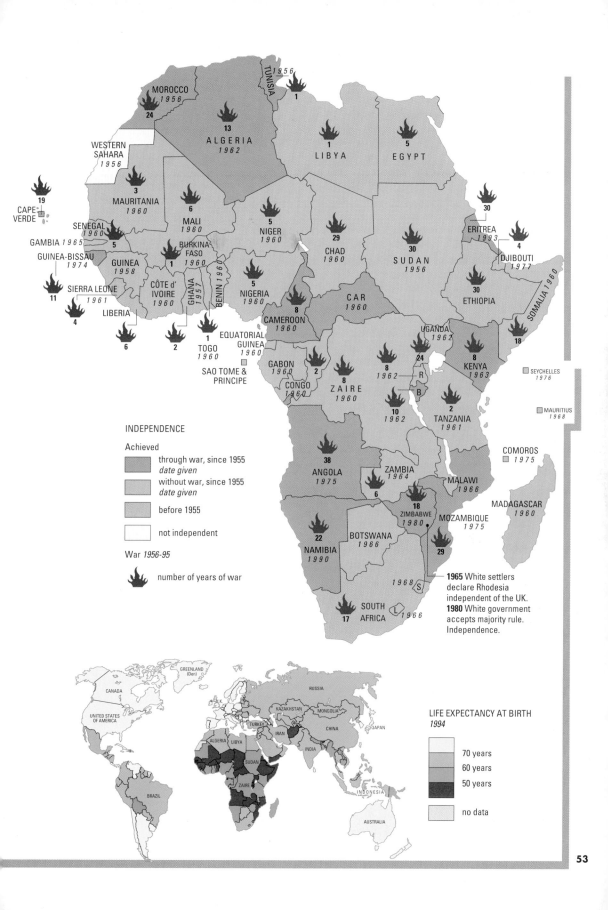

MOROCCO
*1956*
**24**

TUNISIA *1956*
**1**

WESTERN
SAHARA
*1956*

ALGERIA
*1962*
**13**

LIBYA

EGYPT
**5**

CAPE
VERDE
**19**

MAURITANIA
*1960*
**3**

MALI
*1960*
**6**

NIGER
*1960*
**5**

CHAD
*1960*
**29**

SUDAN
*1956*
**30**

ERITREA
*1993*
**30**

DJIBOUTI
*1977*
**4**

SENEGAL
*1960*
**5**

GAMBIA *1965*

GUINEA-BISSAU
*1974*

GUINEA
*1958*

SIERRA LEONE
*1961*
**11**

LIBERIA
**4**

BURKINA
FASO
*1960*

CÔTE d'
IVOIRE
*1960*
**6**

GHANA
*1957*
**2**

BENIN *1960*
**1**

TOGO
*1960*

NIGERIA
*1960*
**5**

CAMEROON
*1960*
**8**

EQUATORIAL
GUINEA
*1960*

SAO TOME &
PRINCIPE

CAR
*1960*

ETHIOPIA
**30**

SOMALIA *1960*

UGANDA
*1962*
**8**

KENYA
*1963*
**8**

SEYCHELLES
*1976*

GABON
*1960*
**2**

CONGO
*1960*

ZAIRE
*1960*
**8**

**24**

R

B

**10**
*1962*

TANZANIA
*1961*
**2**

MAURITIUS
*1968*

COMOROS
*1975*

ANGOLA
*1975*
**38**

ZAMBIA
*1964*

**6**

MALAWI
*1966*

ZIMBABWE
*1980*

MOZAMBIQUE
*1975*
**29**

MADAGASCAR
*1960*

NAMIBIA
*1990*
**22**

BOTSWANA
*1966*

**18**

*1968*
S

SOUTH
AFRICA
*1966*
**17**

L

INDEPENDENCE

Achieved

through war, since 1955
*date given*

without war, since 1955
*date given*

before 1955

not independent

War *1956-95*

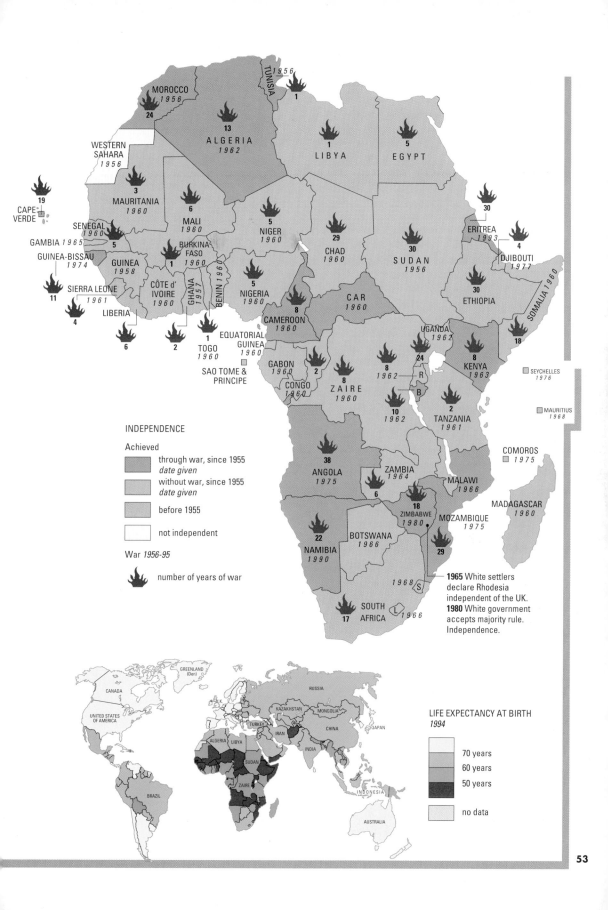  number of years of war

**1965** White settlers
declare Rhodesia
independent of the UK.
**1980** White government
accepts majority rule.
Independence.

LIFE EXPECTANCY AT BIRTH
*1994*

GREENLAND
(Den)

CANADA

UNITED STATES
OF AMERICA

RUSSIA

KAZAKHSTAN

MONGOLIA

TURKEY

IRAN

CHINA

JAPAN

ALGERIA

LIBYA

SUDAN

INDIA

BRAZIL

ZAIRE

INDONESIA

AUSTRALIA

70 years

60 years

50 years

no data

# 19 THE DISPOSSESSED

**West Africa has never recovered from European rule. With fragile economies and no democracies, the region is scarred by poverty, violence and brutality.**

Sierra Leone and Liberia are rich in minerals, timber and dictatorship. In December 1989, the National Patriotic Front of Liberia (NPFL) and the Revolutionary United Front of Sierra Leone (RUF) crossed into northeastern Liberia from Côte d'Ivoire. The NPFL launched a war against Liberia's President Doe. War deaths in 1990 alone amounted to 150,000. In September 1990, Doe was caught and killed. A West African force was sent to keep the peace. When the victors fell out, the peacekeepers joined the fighting against the NPFL; observers say they joined the looting and random violence too.

Eyewitness accounts of a massacre of 500 refugees by a group of teenage fighters in Liberia in June 1993, describe how a five year old boy's head was sawn off; his parents were forced to watch and applaud.

The eleventh agreement to end the war was reached in August 1995. Unemployment stood at 90 percent. In 1996, fighting escalated again.

In March 1991 the RUF moved from Liberia into Sierra Leone. There, in 1992, the military dictator was ousted by a military coup that installed a military dictator who was ousted by a military coup in January 1996. The military prefers not to fight the RUF and only does so when it has no choice. The government uses mercenaries alongside the army: Ghurka Security Guards until 1995, then Executive Outcomes from South Africa, whose rate is reportedly US $500,000 a month.

Both sides, the RUF and Sierra Leone's army, attack civilians. Both sides punish suspected collaborators – or anyone who gets in their way – by cutting off both arms or all fingers.

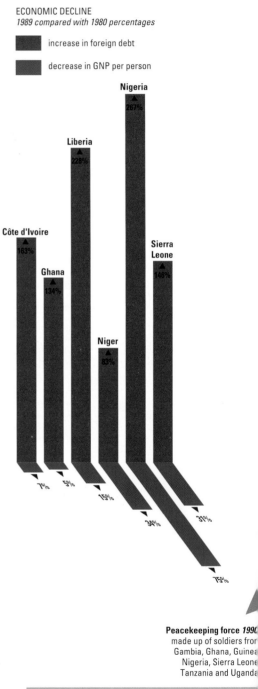

ECONOMIC DECLINE
*1989 compared with 1980 percentages*

██ increase in foreign debt

██ decrease in GNP per person

Nigeria ▲ 267%

Liberia ▲ 228%

Côte d'Ivoire ▲ 163%

Sierra Leone ▲ 146%

Ghana ▲ 134%

Niger ▲ 83%

7%  5%  15%  34%  31%  75%

**Peacekeeping force *1990***
made up of soldiers from
Gambia, Ghana, Guinea
Nigeria, Sierra Leone
Tanzania and Uganda

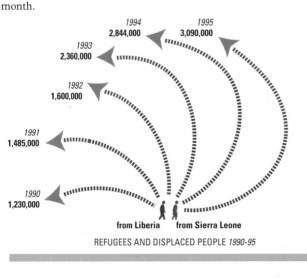

1994
2,844,000

1995
3,090,000

1993
2,360,000

1992
1,600,000

1991
1,485,000

1990
1,230,000

from Liberia     from Sierra Leone

REFUGEES AND DISPLACED PEOPLE *1990-95*

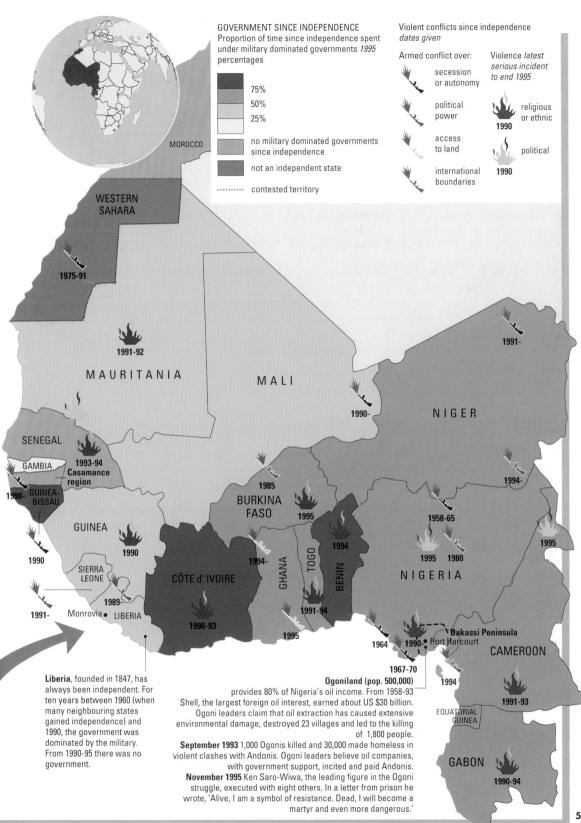

GOVERNMENT SINCE INDEPENDENCE
Proportion of time since independence spent under military dominated governments *1995* percentages

75%
50%
25%

no military dominated governments since independence

not an independent state

.......... contested territory

Violent conflicts since independence
*dates given*

Armed conflict over:

secession or autonomy

political power

access to land

international boundaries

Violence *latest serious incident to end 1995*

religious or ethnic
1990

political
1990

MOROCCO

WESTERN SAHARA

1975-91

MAURITANIA

1991-92

MALI

NIGER

1991-

1990-

SENEGAL

1993-94
Casamance region

GAMBIA

1990-

GUINEA-BISSAU

GUINEA

1990

1985

BURKINA FASO

1995

1994-

1994-

1958-65

1995  1980

1995

1990

SIERRA LEONE

1989

1991-

Monrovia  LIBERIA

CÔTE d' IVOIRE

1990-93

GHANA

TOGO

BENIN

1991-94

1995

NIGERIA

Bakassi Peninsula
Port Harcourt

1964  1990

1967-70

1994

CAMEROON

1991-93

EQUATORIAL GUINEA

GABON

1990-94

**Liberia**, founded in 1847, has always been independent. For ten years between 1960 (when many neighbouring states gained independence) and 1990, the government was dominated by the military. From 1990-95 there was no government.

**Ogoniland (pop. 500,000)** provides 80% of Nigeria's oil income. From 1958-93 Shell, the largest foreign oil interest, earned about US $30 billion. Ogoni leaders claim that oil extraction has caused extensive environmental damage, destroyed 23 villages and led to the killing of 1,800 people.
**September 1993** 1,000 Ogonis killed and 30,000 made homeless in violent clashes with Andonis. Ogoni leaders believe oil companies, with government support, incited and paid Andonis.
**November 1995** Ken Saro-Wiwa, the leading figure in the Ogoni struggle, executed with eight others. In a letter from prison he wrote, 'Alive, I am a symbol of resistance. Dead, I will become a martyr and even more dangerous.'

55

# 20 TIMES FOR KILLING

**The people of Burundi and Rwanda, and most of their neighbouring countries, have suffered more than three decades of war, repression, uprising and massacre since independence.**

In Rwanda, the majority ethnic group are the Hutus, the minority are Tutsis. Since independence, most of the rulers have been Hutu. In Burundi, at the time of independence, Hutus were also the majority, but the army and the ruling groups since independence have been almost exclusively Tutsi. In both countries, land scarcity combines explosively with ethnic rivalry. Economic weakness compounds the problem. In 1989 world coffee prices fell by 50 percent. Rwanda lost 40 percent of its export income and faced the worst food shortages for fifty years. International loans were spent on military equipment while public services collapsed.

In October 1990, the Rwanda Patriotic Front (RPF) invaded Rwanda from Uganda. The RPF is made up of Tutsi exiles, many of whom had been driven off their land by Hutus backed by the army.

Throughout the late 1980s and early 1990s, Burundi also experienced violent conflict. In 1993, peace agreements were adopted in both countries. In Burundi, the largely Hutu Front for Democracy won elections and formed a government. The army was left in Tutsi hands. In Rwanda, a transitional government was made up of Hutus and Tutsis. But by 1994, the Hutu militias who had been equipped and trained by Rwandan security forces, claimed they could kill 1,000 Tutsis in any period of 20 minutes.

Burundi broke first. President Melchior Ndadaye was assassinated in an army uprising in October 1993. Massacres and counter massacres started, killing 150,000 people. There were 200 killings a week in Burundi in 1995, according to UN estimates. Rwanda's massacres began in April 1994, triggered by the death of General Juvénal Habyarimana in a plane crash and by the RPF's steady progress towards victory. In 1996 over 50,000 prisoners awaited trial as war criminals.

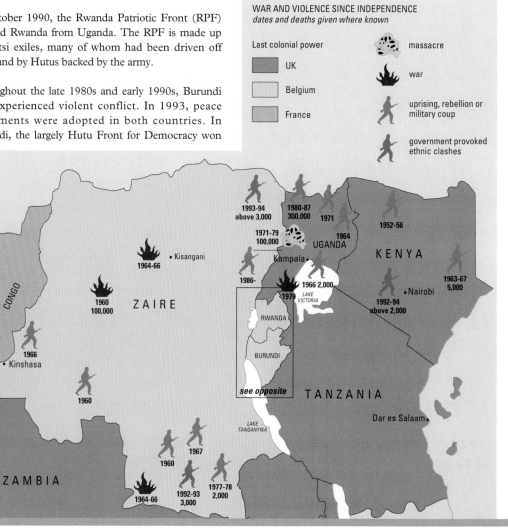

WAR AND VIOLENCE SINCE INDEPENDENCE
*dates and deaths given where known*

Last colonial power

UK

Belgium

France

massacre

war

uprising, rebellion or military coup

government provoked ethnic clashes

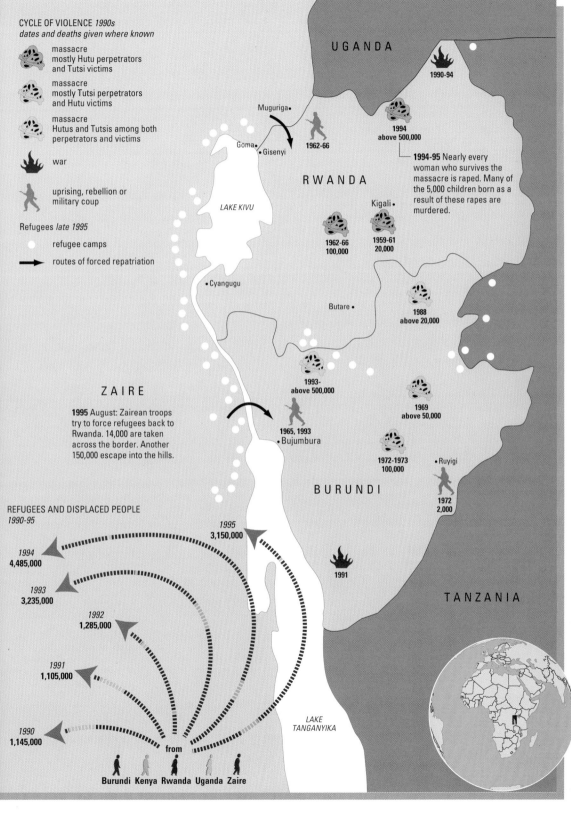

CYCLE OF VIOLENCE *1990s*
*dates and deaths given where known*

massacre
mostly Hutu perpetrators
and Tutsi victims

massacre
mostly Tutsi perpetrators
and Hutu victims

massacre
Hutus and Tutsis among both
perpetrators and victims

war

uprising, rebellion or
military coup

Refugees *late 1995*

refugee camps

routes of forced repatriation

UGANDA

1990-94

Muguriga•

Goma•
•Gisenyi

1962-66

1994
above 500,000

RWANDA

**1994-95** Nearly every
woman who survives the
massacre is raped. Many of
the 5,000 children born as a
result of these rapes are
murdered.

*LAKE KIVU*

Kigali•

1962-66
100,000

1959-61
20,000

•Cyangugu

Butare •

1988
above 20,000

ZAIRE

**1995** August: Zairean troops
try to force refugees back to
Rwanda. 14,000 are taken
across the border. Another
150,000 escape into the hills.

1993-
above 500,000

1969
above 50,000

1965, 1993
•Bujumbura

1972-1973
100,000

•Ruyigi

1972
2,000

BURUNDI

1991

TANZANIA

REFUGEES AND DISPLACED PEOPLE
*1990-95*

*1994*
4,485,000

*1993*
3,235,000

*1992*
1,285,000

*1991*
1,105,000

*1990*
1,145,000

*1995*
3,150,000

*LAKE
TANGANYIKA*

from

Burundi  Kenya  Rwanda  Uganda  Zaire

Dan Smith *The State of War and Peace Atlas* 3rd edition Copyright © Myriad Editions Limited

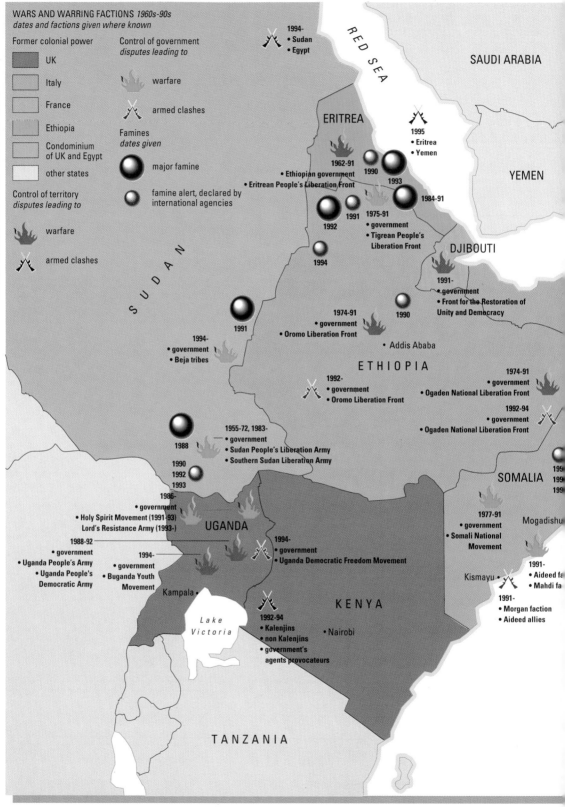

**WARS AND WARRING FACTIONS** *1960s-90s*
*dates and factions given where known*

Former colonial power
- UK
- Italy
- France
- Ethiopia
- Condominium of UK and Egypt
- other states

Control of territory
*disputes leading to*
- warfare
- armed clashes

Control of government
*disputes leading to*
- warfare
- armed clashes

Famines
*dates given*
- major famine
- famine alert, declared by international agencies

RED SEA

SAUDI ARABIA

1994-
- Sudan
- Egypt

ERITREA

1995
- Eritrea
- Yemen

YEMEN

1962-91
- Ethiopian government
- Eritrean People's Liberation Front

1990

1993

1984-91

1991

1975-91
- government
- Tigrean People's Liberation Front

1992

1994

DJIBOUTI

1991-
- government
- Front for the Restoration of Unity and Democracy

1974-91
- government
- Oromo Liberation Front

1990

S U D A N

1991

1994-
- government
- Beja tribes

- Addis Ababa

E T H I O P I A

1992-
- government
- Oromo Liberation Front

1974-91
- government
- Ogaden National Liberation Front

1992-94
- government
- Ogaden National Liberation Front

1988

1955-72, 1983-
- government
- Sudan People's Liberation Army
- Southern Sudan Liberation Army

1990
1992
1993

SOMALIA

199
199
199

1977-91
- government
- Somali National Movement

Mogadishu

1986-
- government
- Holy Spirit Movement (1991-93)
  Lord's Resistance Army (1993-)

1988-92
- government
- Uganda People's Army
- Uganda People's Democratic Army

1994-
- government
- Buganda Youth Movement

UGANDA

1994-
- government
- Uganda Democratic Freedom Movement

1991-
- Aideed fa
- Mahdi fa

Kismayu

1991-
- Morgan faction
- Aideed allies

Kampala

Lake Victoria

K E N Y A

1992-94
- Kalenjins
- non Kalenjins
- government's agents provocateurs

Nairobi

T A N Z A N I A

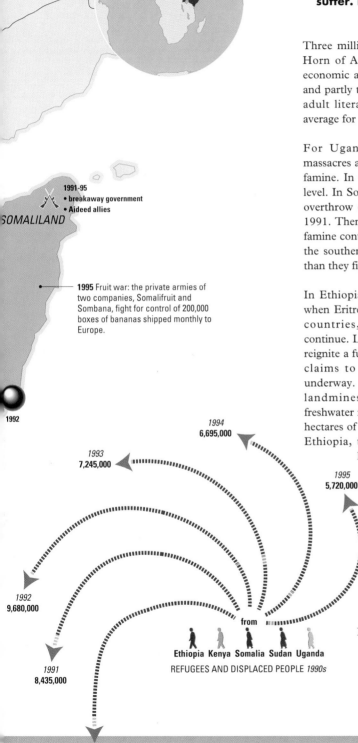

**War and poverty are midwives to each other. In the Horn of Africa, rebels divide into factions, states disintegrate and people suffer. Ethiopia and Eritrea have a chance for something better.**

Three million people have died in the wars of the Horn of Africa since the early 1960s. Desperate economic and social conditions are partly the cause and partly the result of the warfare. Life expectancy, adult literacy and income are all well below the average for the Third World.

For Uganda, the 1970s were dominated by massacres and repression, the 1980s by civil war and famine. In the 1990s, civil war continues at a lower level. In Somalia, 14 years of war brought about the overthrow of the dictator, President Siad Barre, in 1991. Then the victors fell out, and the fighting and famine continued. In Sudan different factions among the southern rebels fight each other more intensely than they fight the northern government.

In Ethiopia, three decades of war ended in 1991 when Eritrea became an independent state. In both countries, poverty is still acute and tensions continue. Low level violence in Ethiopia threatens to reignite a full scale war and Eritrea contests Yemen's claims to the Red Sea. Yet reconstruction is underway. Both governments have started to clear landmines. Eritrea has built micro dams and freshwater reservoirs, dug wells, prepared over 2,000 hectares of cropland and planted millions of trees. In Ethiopia, the government plans to build 11,000 kilometres of road by the year 2000. Arms factories now make civilian goods. A bonus has been the discovery of a large natural gas field in eastern Ethiopia.

The war years cannot yet be forgotten. In the mid 1990s, 44 members of the pre 1991 government in Ethiopia are on trial, charged with torture, crimes against humanity and genocide, including the murder of 2,000 political opponents. The penalty could be death. How these trials are handled – whether on the basis of justice or revenge – is a major test for peacemakers in Ethiopia.

**SOMALILAND**

**1991-95**
• breakaway government
• Aideed allies

**1995** Fruit war: the private armies of two companies, Somalifruit and Sombana, fight for control of 200,000 boxes of bananas shipped monthly to Europe.

*1992*

*1994*
**6,695,000**

*1993*
**7,245,000**

*1995*
**5,720,000**

*1992*
**9,680,000**

**from**

Ethiopia Kenya Somalia Sudan Uganda
REFUGEES AND DISPLACED PEOPLE *1990s*

*1991*
**8,435,000**

*1990*
**8,225,000**

**Southeast Asia has been a region of war, terror and repression since the Second World War.**

There have been three overlapping waves of armed conflict in Southeast Asia since 1945. First came decolonization and its immediate aftermath. In Vietnam alone, 600,000 people were killed between 1945 and 1954 during its war of independence from France. When Portugal moved out of East Timor in 1975, the island was claimed and occupied by Indonesia, whose forces killed 15 percent of the Timorese population.

The second wave of armed conflict was part of the Cold War. Nearly two and a half million people died in Vietnam between 1960 and 1975. Over one million people – perhaps over three million – have died in Cambodia since 1970 in a conflict that is still not finally settled. Half a million Indonesian Communists were massacred in 1966.

The third wave of armed conflict is over control of

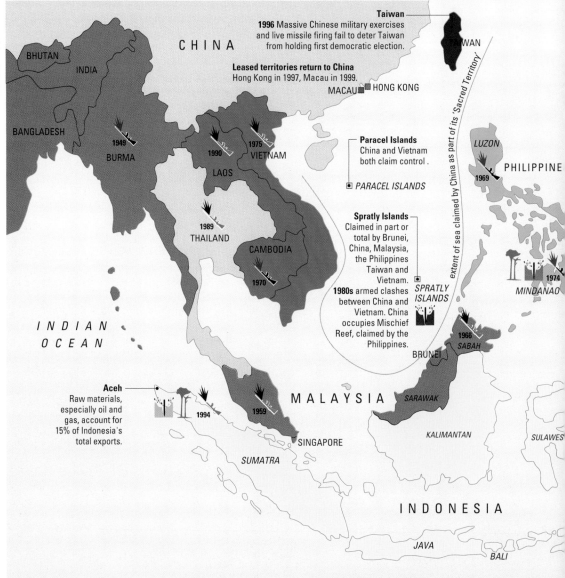

**Taiwan**
1996 Massive Chinese military exercises and live missile firing fail to deter Taiwan from holding first democratic election.

**Leased territories return to China**
Hong Kong in 1997, Macau in 1999.

**Paracel Islands**
China and Vietnam both claim control .

**Spratly Islands**
Claimed in part or total by Brunei, China, Malaysia, the Philippines Taiwan and Vietnam.
1980s armed clashes between China and Vietnam. China occupies Mischief Reef, claimed by the Philippines.

**Aceh**
Raw materials, especially oil and gas, account for 15% of Indonesia's total exports.

extent of sea claimed by China as part of its 'Sacred Territory'

CHINA
BHUTAN
INDIA
BANGLADESH
BURMA
VIETNAM
LAOS
THAILAND
CAMBODIA
MACAU  HONG KONG
TAIWAN
LUZON
PHILIPPINE
PARACEL ISLANDS
SPRATLY ISLANDS
MINDANAO
SABAH
BRUNEI
SARAWAK
KALIMANTAN
SULAWES
INDIAN OCEAN
MALAYSIA
SINGAPORE
SUMATRA
INDONESIA
JAVA
BALI

1949
1990
1975
1969
1989
1970
1974
1966
1994
1959

natural resources. Parties divide on ethnic or religious lines and fight for forests, gold and copper. In the Philippines, Islamist insurgents claim to control about half the naturally rich island of Mindanao. In Bougainville, an island of 200,000 people, insurgents object to the fact that Papua New Guinea takes 95 percent of the income from the island's Panaguna copper mine. In Irian Jaya, three decades of armed struggle for independence prevent the Indonesian government and multinational corporations from fully exploiting the island's major natural resource – the world's largest active gold mine.

Beneath the sea lie untapped oil reserves. Oil persuades the Australian government to turn a blind eye to Indonesia's otherwise widely condemned occupation of East Timor. Oil lends a modern urgency to China's claim that the whole of the South China Sea is part of its 'Sacred Territory'. And oil helps to explain why every other state in the region contests the Chinese claim.

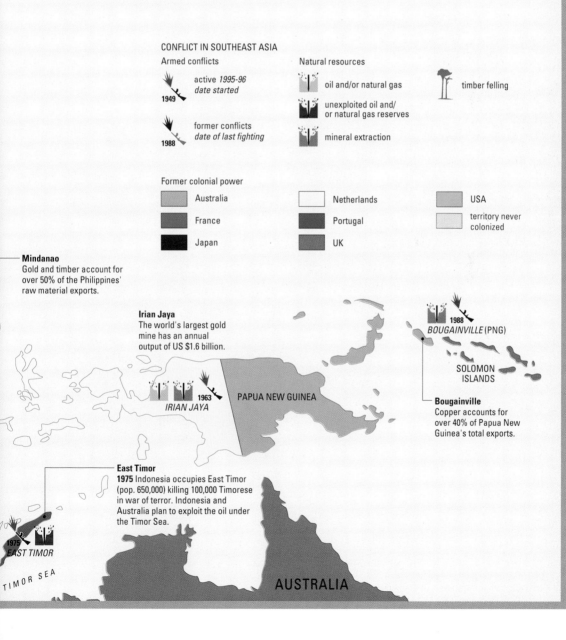

CONFLICT IN SOUTHEAST ASIA

Armed conflicts

active 1995-96
date started
1949

former conflicts
date of last fighting
1988

Natural resources

oil and/or natural gas

unexploited oil and/
or natural gas reserves

mineral extraction

timber felling

Former colonial power

Australia

France

Japan

Netherlands

Portugal

UK

USA

territory never
colonized

Mindanao
Gold and timber account for over 50% of the Philippines' raw material exports.

Irian Jaya
The world's largest gold mine has an annual output of US $1.6 billion.

IRIAN JAYA
1963

PAPUA NEW GUINEA

1988
BOUGAINVILLE (PNG)

SOLOMON ISLANDS

Bougainville
Copper accounts for over 40% of Papua New Guinea's total exports.

East Timor
1975 Indonesia occupies East Timor (pop. 650,000) killing 100,000 Timorese in war of terror. Indonesia and Australia plan to exploit the oil under the Timor Sea.

1975
EAST TIMOR

TIMOR SEA

AUSTRALIA

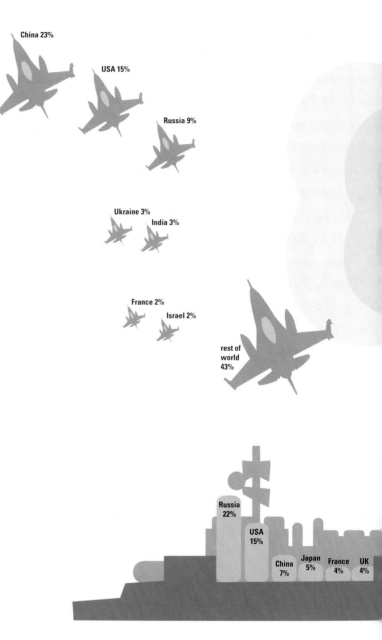

China 23%

USA 15%

Russia 9%

Ukraine 3%

India 3%

France 2%

Israel 2%

rest of
world
43%

Russia
22%

USA
15%

China
7%

Japan
5%

France
4%

UK
4%

STATES' SHARES OF WARSHIPS,
BATTLE TANKS, COMBAT AIRCRAFT *1995*
AND NUCLEAR TESTS *to 1995*
percentages

There are 120,000 battle tanks,
35,000 combat aircraft and
1,500 major warships worldwide.
Compared to 1989, the last year of the Cold War,
there are now 25 percent fewer warships,
20 percent fewer tanks and 15 percent fewer combat aircraft.
Ownership is concentrated in a few states.
Over 2,000 nuclear tests have been conducted since the first in 1945.

USA
51%

former USSR
35%

France
10%

UK, China
2%

India
0.05%

Ukraine 4%
Syria 4%
Israel 3%
Egypt 3%
North Korea 3%
Cuba 3%

China
7%

USA
10%

Russia
17%

rest of world
46%

**Over 23 million people are in regular and irregular armed forces. They include over half a million women and 200,000 children under 15.**

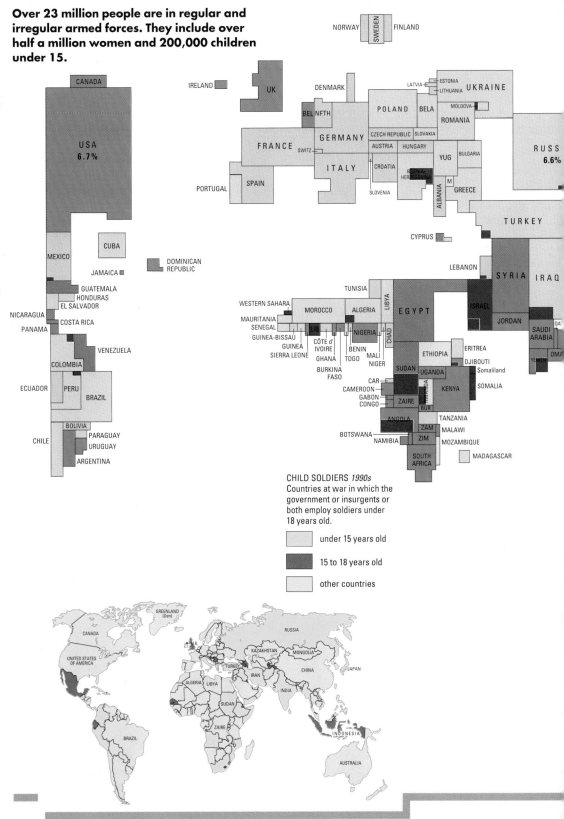

NORWAY  SWEDEN  FINLAND

CANADA

IRELAND  UK  DENMARK  LATVIA  ESTONIA  UKRAINE  LITHUANIA

BEL  NFTH  POLAND  BELA  MOLDOVA  ROMANIA

USA
6.7%

FRANCE  GERMANY  CZECH REPUBLIC  SLOVAKIA
SWITZ  AUSTRIA  HUNGARY  RUSS
ITALY  CROATIA  YUG  BULGARIA  6.6%
SLOVENIA  BOSNIA-HERZEGOVINA  M  ALBANIA  GREECE

PORTUGAL  SPAIN

TURKEY

MEXICO  CUBA  DOMINICAN REPUBLIC
JAMAICA

CYPRUS

LEBANON  SYRIA  IRAQ

GUATEMALA  HONDURAS  EL SALVADOR  TUNISIA  LIBYA  ISRAEL
NICARAGUA  WESTERN SAHARA  MOROCCO  ALGERIA  EGYPT  JORDAN  QA
COSTA RICA  MAURITANIA  SAUDI ARABIA
PANAMA  SENEGAL  LIB  NIGERIA  CHAD  OMA
VENEZUELA  GUINEA-BISSAU  CÔTE d'IVOIRE  YEMEN
COLOMBIA  GUINEA  SIERRA LEONE  GHANA  TOGO  MALI NIGER  ETHIOPIA  ERITREA  DJIBOUTI
BENIN  Somaliland
ECUADOR  PERU  BRAZIL  BURKINA FASO  SUDAN  UGANDA
CAR  KENYA  SOMALIA
CAMEROON  RWANDA
GABON  ZAIRE
BOLIVIA  CONGO  BUR
CHILE  PARAGUAY  ANGOLA  TANZANIA
URUGUAY  ZAM  MALAWI
ARGENTINA  BOTSWANA  NAMIBIA  ZIM  MOZAMBIQUE  MADAGASCAR
SOUTH AFRICA

**CHILD SOLDIERS** *1990s*
Countries at war in which the government or insurgents or both employ soldiers under 18 years old.

| | |
|---|---|
| | under 15 years old |
| | 15 to 18 years old |
| | other countries |

GREENLAND (Den)
CANADA  RUSSIA
KAZAKHSTAN  MONGOLIA
UNITED STATES OF AMERICA  TURKEY  JAPAN
IRAN  CHINA
ALGERIA LIBYA  INDIA
SUDAN  INDONESIA
BRAZIL  ZAIRE
AUSTRALIA

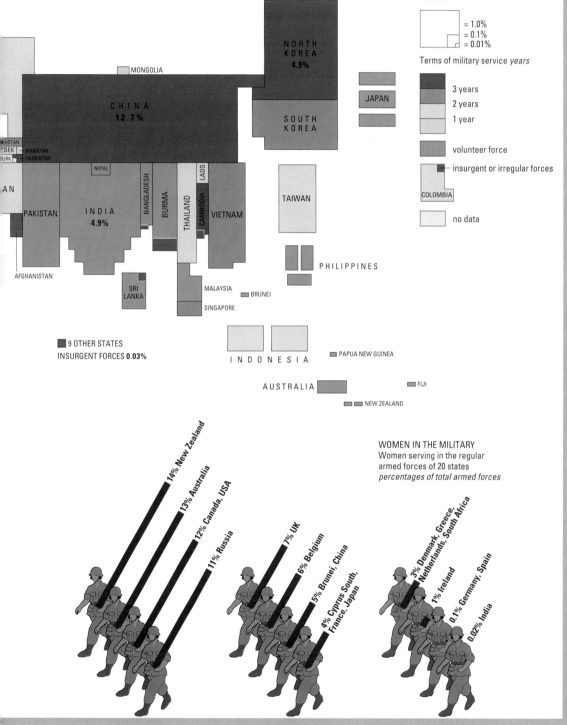

ARMED FORCES
States' shares of military personnel
worldwide *1994* percentages

states of 3% or over: percentage given
states or forces under 0.01%:
not shown

= 1.0%
= 0.1%
= 0.01%

Terms of military service *years*

3 years
2 years
1 year

volunteer force

insurgent or irregular forces

COLOMBIA

no data

MONGOLIA

NORTH KOREA
4.9%

JAPAN

CHINA
12.7%

SOUTH KOREA

KHSTAN
ʻBEK    KIRGISTAN
URK    TAJIKISTAN

NEPAL

LAOS

TAIWAN

A N

PAKISTAN

INDIA
4.9%

BANGLADESH

BURMA

THAILAND

CAMBODIA

VIETNAM

AFGHANISTAN

SRI LANKA

MALAYSIA

BRUNEI

SINGAPORE

PHILIPPINES

9 OTHER STATES
INSURGENT FORCES **0.03%**

INDONESIA

PAPUA NEW GUINEA

AUSTRALIA

FIJI

NEW ZEALAND

14% New Zealand
13% Australia
12% Canada, USA
11% Russia

7% UK
6% Belgium
5% Brunei, China
4% Cyprus South, France, Japan

3% Denmark, Greece, Netherlands, South Africa
1% Ireland
0.1% Germany, Spain
0.02% India

WOMEN IN THE MILITARY
Women serving in the regular
armed forces of 20 states
*percentages of total armed forces*

65

# 24 MILITARY SPENDING

In the mid 1990s, known military spending was US $800 billion each year — or US $145 per person worldwide. This is 30 percent less than in 1985, the height of the Cold War.

THE PEACE DIVIDEND
Annual saving in military spending *1990-91,* and projected *1995-99*
US $ billion

$29b    $58b    $86b    $113b    $140b

**1990-94**

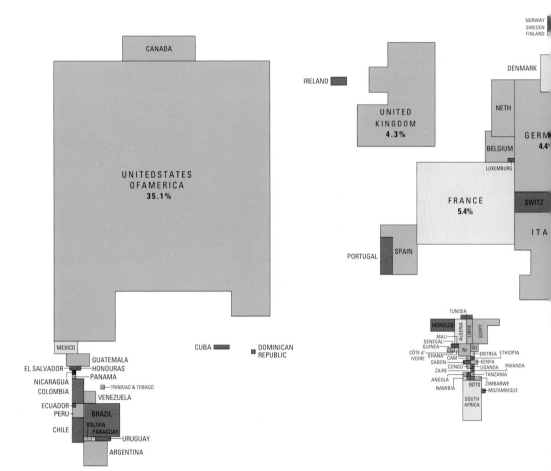

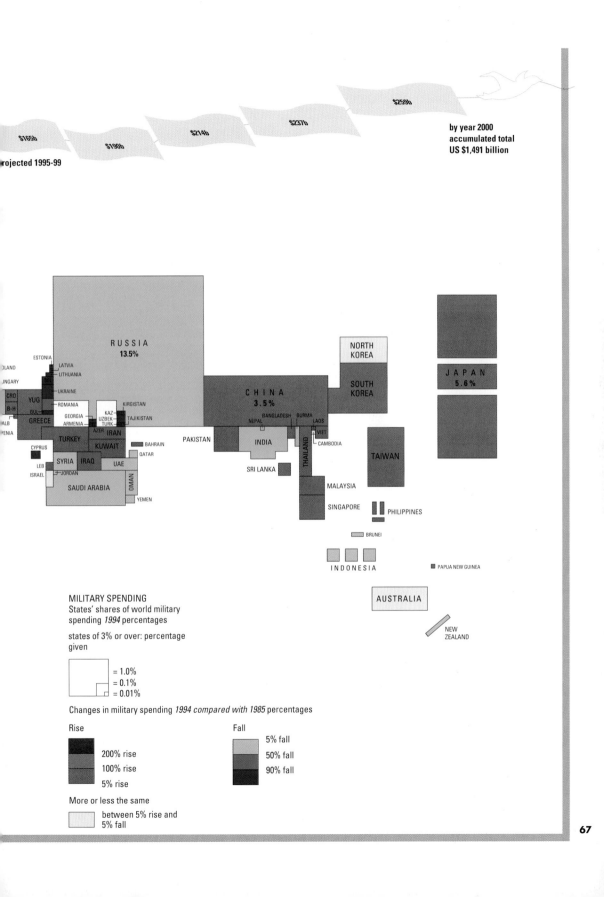

$165b

projected 1995-99

$190b

$214b

$237b

$259b

by year 2000
accumulated total
US $1,491 billion

RUSSIA
13.5%

ESTONIA
POLAND
HUNGARY
LATVIA
LITHUANIA
BUL
UKRAINE
CRO
YUG
B-H
ROMANIA
ALB
GREECE
GEORGIA
ARMENIA
KAZ
UZBEK
TURK
KIRGISTAN
TAJIKISTAN
ARMENIA
AZER
IRAN
CYPRUS
TURKEY
KUWAIT
BAHRAIN
LEB
ISRAEL
SYRIA
IRAQ
JORDAN
QATAR
UAE
OMAN
SAUDI ARABIA
YEMEN

PAKISTAN

NEPAL
INDIA
BANGLADESH
BURMA
SRI LANKA

THAILAND
LAOS
VIET
CAMBODIA

CHINA
3.5%

NORTH
KOREA

SOUTH
KOREA

TAIWAN

MALAYSIA

SINGAPORE

PHILIPPINES

BRUNEI

INDONESIA

PAPUA NEW GUINEA

JAPAN
5.6%

AUSTRALIA

NEW
ZEALAND

MILITARY SPENDING
States' shares of world military
spending *1994* percentages

states of 3% or over: percentage
given

= 1.0%
= 0.1%
= 0.01%

Changes in military spending *1994 compared with 1985* percentages

Rise

200% rise

100% rise

5% rise

Fall

5% fall

50% fall

90% fall

More or less the same

between 5% rise and
5% fall

# 25 MARKET FORCES

In 1994, the value of world trade in major
weapons was US $22 billion, less than half
its value in 1985. The value of world trade
in light weapons, such as handguns, is
unknown and uncontrollable.

Dan Smith *The State of War and Peace Atlas* 3rd edition Copyright © Myriad Editions Limited

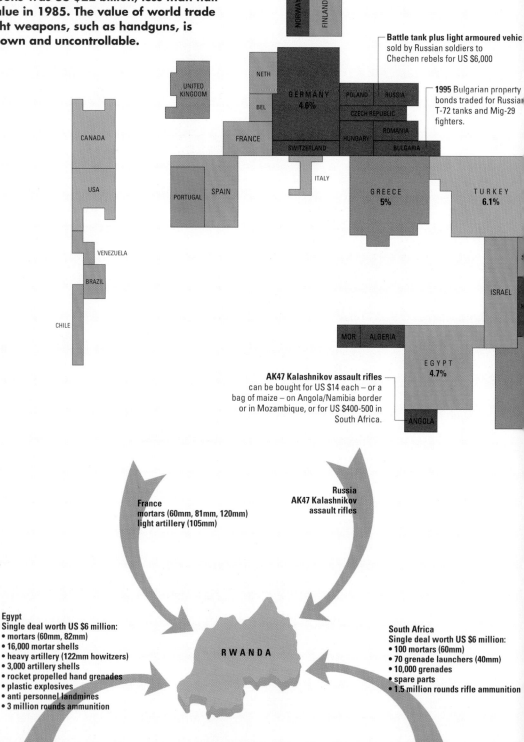

**Battle tank plus light armoured vehic**
sold by Russian soldiers to
Chechen rebels for US $6,000

**1995** Bulgarian property
bonds traded for Russian
T-72 tanks and Mig-29
fighters.

**AK47 Kalashnikov assault rifles**
can be bought for US $14 each – or a
bag of maize – on Angola/Namibia border
or in Mozambique, or for US $400-500 in
South Africa.

NORWAY   FINLAND

NETH
UNITED
KINGDOM
GERMANY
4.6%
POLAND   RUSSIA
BEL
CZECH REPUBLIC
CANADA
FRANCE
HUNGARY   ROMANIA
SWITZERLAND   BULGARIA
USA
ITALY
PORTUGAL   SPAIN
GREECE
5%
TURKEY
6.1%
VENEZUELA
BRAZIL
ISRAEL
CHILE
MOR   ALGERIA
EGYPT
4.7%
ANGOLA

France
mortars (60mm, 81mm, 120mm)
light artillery (105mm)

Russia
AK47 Kalashnikov
assault rifles

**Egypt**
**Single deal worth US $6 million:**
• mortars (60mm, 82mm)
• 16,000 mortar shells
• heavy artillery (122mm howitzers)
• 3,000 artillery shells
• rocket propelled hand grenades
• plastic explosives
• anti personnel landmines
• 3 million rounds ammunition

RWANDA

**South Africa**
**Single deal worth US $6 million:**
• 100 mortars (60mm)
• 70 grenade launchers (40mm)
• 10,000 grenades
• spare parts
• 1.5 million rounds rifle ammunition

ARMING RWANDA *1990-94*

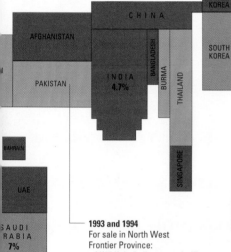

AFGHANISTAN

PAKISTAN

CHINA

BANGLADESH

INDIA
4.7%

BURMA

THAILAND

SINGAPORE

BAHRAIN

UAE

SAUDI
ARABIA
7%

NORTH
KOREA

SOUTH
KOREA

JAPAN
6.6%

TAIWAN
3%

INDONESIA

AUSTRALIA

**1993 and 1994**
For sale in North West
Frontier Province:
• AK47 Kalashnikov assault rifles
• and Chinese copies
• sniper rifles
• rocket propelled grenades
• recoilless anti tank rifles
• Chinese 122 mm artillery rockets

ARMS IMPORTERS *1990-94*
States' shares of world imports of
major conventional weapons
percentages

states of 3% or over: percentage given

= 1.0%

= 0.1%

Change in value of imports of major
conventional weapons *1990-94*

300% increase

100% increase

50% decrease

GREENLAND
(Den)

CANADA

ALK.

UNITED STATES OF AMERICA

BRAZIL

ALGERIA

LIBYA

SUDAN

ZAIRE

TURKEY

IRAN

KAZAKHSTAN

MONGOLIA

CHINA

JAPAN

INDIA

INDONESIA

AUSTRALIA

ARMS EXPORTERS *1990-94*
Top 24 states' shares of world exports
of major conventional weapons
percentages

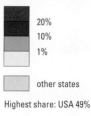

20%

10%

1%

other states

Highest share: USA 49%

**69**

**The threat of ABC weapons — atomic, biological, chemical — has haunted world security since 1945 but their use has been limited.**

Dan Smith *The State of War and Peace Atlas* 3rd edition Copyright © Myriad Editions Limited

GREENLAND (Den)

ICELAND

CANADA

NORWAY  SWEDEN

IRELAND  UNITED KINGDOM  DEN
NETH  GERMANY  POL
BELG  CZECH
FRANCE  AUS
ITALY

PORTUGAL  SPAIN

UNITED STATES OF AMERICA

MEXICO  CUBA
DOMINICAN REPUBLIC
BELIZE  JAMAICA  HAITI
GUATEMALA
EL SALVADOR  NICARAGUA
HONDURAS
COSTA RICA
PANAMA  VENEZUELA  GUYANA
COLOMBIA  SURINAME
FRENCH GUIANA (Fr)
ECUADOR

PERU  BRAZIL
BOLIVIA
PARAGUAY
CHILE
URUGUAY
ARGENTINA

FALKLAND ISLANDS (UK)

MOROCCO  TUNISIA
WESTERN SAHARA  ALGERIA  LI
MAURITANIA  MALI  NIGER
SENEGAL
GAMBIA  BURKINA FASO
GUINEA-BISSAU  GUINEA  NIGERIA
SIERRA LEONE  CÔTE d'IVOIRE  GHANA  BENIN
LIBERIA  TOGO  CAMEROON
EQUATORIAL GUINEA
GABON
CONGO

ANG
NAMIB

Since 1945, the only proven use of chemical gas weapons is by Egypt in Yemen in the mid 1960s, and by Iraq against Iran and against Kurdish villages in 1988.

## MISSILES AND NUCLEAR WEAPONS *1995*

States owning ballistic missiles with a range of:

- 1,500 kms and more
- 300-1,500 kms
- 40-300 kms
- other states or territory

states owning nuclear weapons

states owning nuclear weapons material

States that have abandoned advanced nuclear weapons programmes

voluntarily

under compulsion

**Nuclear Non Proliferation Treaty**
Under this treaty, states agree to renounce nuclear weapons.

states not party to the Nuclear Non Proliferation Treaty

## NUCLEAR WARHEADS *1995*

Between 1985 and 1996 the number of nuclear warheads worldwide fell from over 50,000 to 20,000. Belarus, Kazakhstan and Ukraine 'inherited' nuclear weapons from the former USSR and are dismantling them.

11,000 Russia
8,500 USA
1,500 Ukraine
650 Kazakhstan
500 France
300 China, UK
100 Israel
36 Belarus

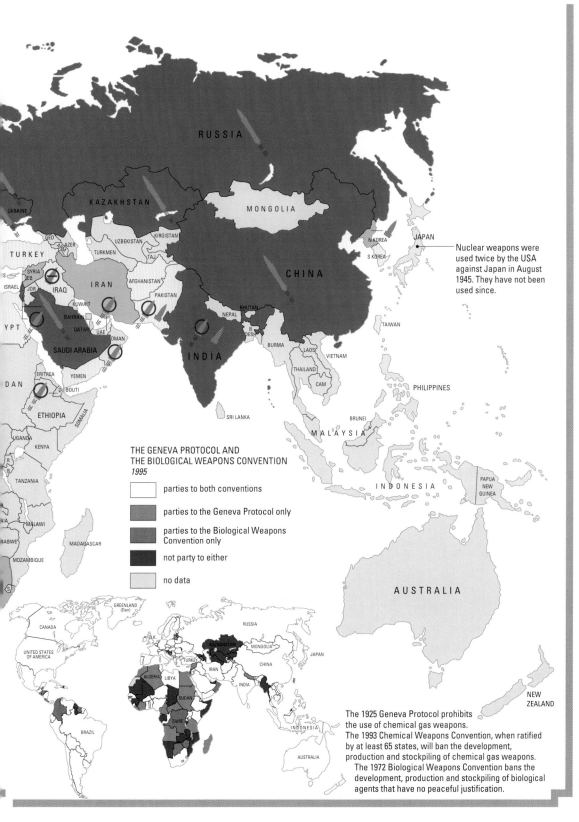

Nuclear weapons were used twice by the USA against Japan in August 1945. They have not been used since.

THE GENEVA PROTOCOL AND
THE BIOLOGICAL WEAPONS CONVENTION
*1995*

parties to both conventions

parties to the Geneva Protocol only

parties to the Biological Weapons Convention only

not party to either

no data

The 1925 Geneva Protocol prohibits
the use of chemical gas weapons.
The 1993 Chemical Weapons Convention, when ratified
by at least 65 states, will ban the development,
production and stockpiling of chemical gas weapons.
The 1972 Biological Weapons Convention bans the
development, production and stockpiling of biological
agents that have no peaceful justification.

# 27 DUMPING GROUNDS

Over two thousand nuclear tests have been
conducted since the first one in 1945. But they
are only one way in which the Cold War polluted
the planet. The clean up has barely begun.

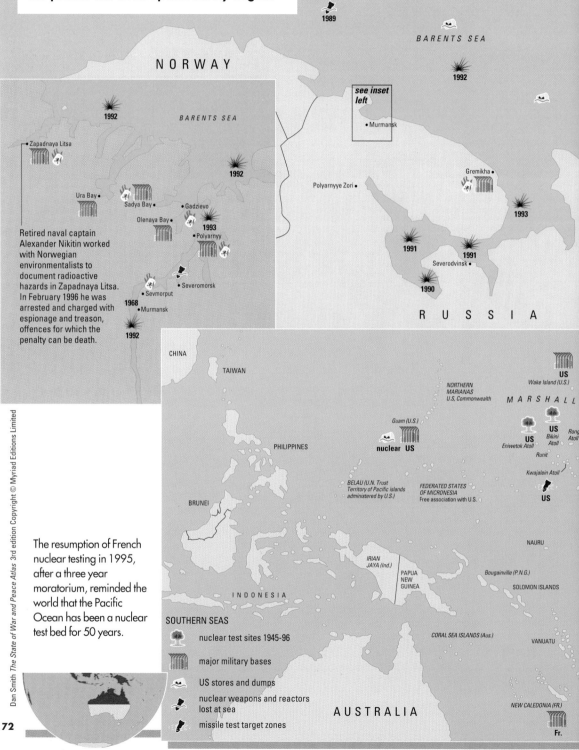

Retired naval captain
Alexander Nikitin worked
with Norwegian
environmentalists to
document radioactive
hazards in Zapadnaya Litsa.
In February 1996 he was
arrested and charged with
espionage and treason,
offences for which the
penalty can be death.

The resumption of French
nuclear testing in 1995,
after a three year
moratorium, reminded the
world that the Pacific
Ocean has been a nuclear
test bed for 50 years.

NORWAY

BARENTS SEA

1989

1992

see inset
left

• Murmansk

1992

BARENTS SEA

1992

• Zapadnaya Litsa

Ura Bay •

Sadya Bay •

• Gadzievo

Olenaya Bay •

1993
• Polyarnyy

• Severomorsk

• Sevmorput

1968
• Murmansk

1992

Polyarnyye Zori •

Gremikha •

1993

1991

1991

Severodvinsk •

1990

RUSSIA

CHINA

TAIWAN

NORTHERN
MARIANAS
U.S, Commonwealth

US
Wake Island (U.S.)

MARSHALL

Guam (U.S.)

PHILIPPINES

nuclear US

US
Eniwetok Atoll

US
Bikini
Atoll

Ronge

Runit

Kwajalein Atoll

US

BELAU (U.N. Trust
Territory of Pacific islands
administered by U.S.)

FEDERATED STATES
OF MICRONESIA
Free association with U.S.

BRUNEI

NAURU

IRIAN
JAYA (Ind.)

PAPUA
NEW
GUINEA

Bougainville (P.N.G.)

SOLOMON ISLANDS

INDONESIA

CORAL SEA ISLANDS (Aus.)

VANUATU

SOUTHERN SEAS

nuclear test sites 1945-96

major military bases

US stores and dumps

nuclear weapons and reactors
lost at sea

missile test target zones

AUSTRALIA

NEW CALEDONIA (FR.)

Fr.

Dan Smith The State of War and Peace Atlas 3rd edition Copyright © Myriad Editions Limited

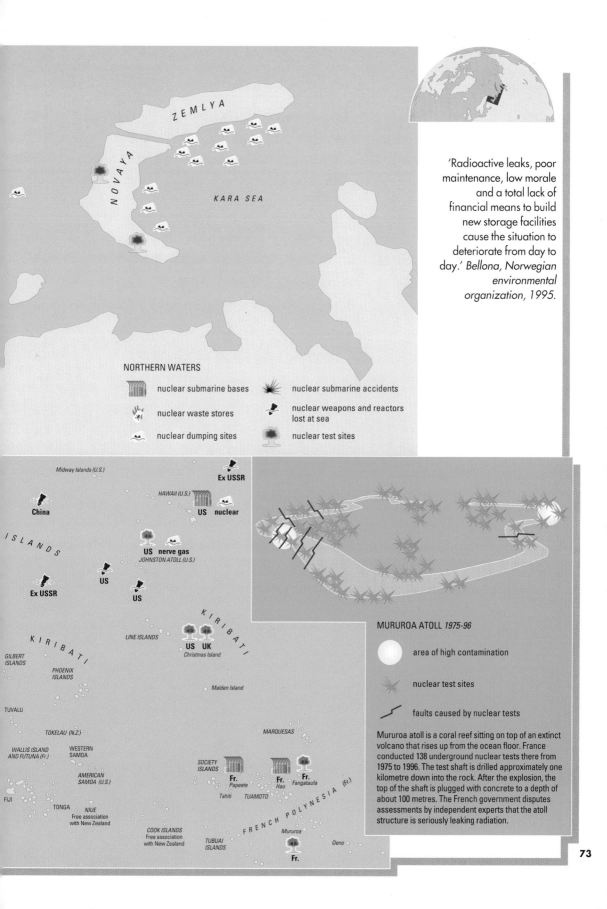

ZEMLYA

NOVAYA

KARA SEA

## NORTHERN WATERS

- nuclear submarine bases
- nuclear waste stores
- nuclear dumping sites
- nuclear submarine accidents
- nuclear weapons and reactors lost at sea
- nuclear test sites

Midway Islands (U.S.)

**Ex USSR**

HAWAII (U.S.)

**China**

**US** nuclear

*ISLANDS*

**US** nerve gas
JOHNSTON ATOLL (U.S.)

**Ex USSR**

**US**

**US**

*KIRIBATI*

LINE ISLANDS

*KIRIBATI*

**US** **UK**
Christmas Island

GILBERT
ISLANDS

PHOENIX
ISLANDS

Malden Island

TUVALU

MARQUESAS

TOKELAU (N.Z.)

WALLIS ISLAND
AND FUTUNA (Fr.)

WESTERN
SAMOA

SOCIETY
ISLANDS

AMERICAN
SAMOA (U.S.)

**Fr.**
Papeete

**Fr.**
Hao

**Fr.**
Fangataufa

FIJI

Tahiti

TUAMOTO

TONGA

NIUE
Free association
with New Zealand

*FRENCH POLYNESIA* (Fr.)

COOK ISLANDS
Free association
with New Zealand

Mururoa

TUBUAI
ISLANDS

Oeno

**Fr.**

## MURUROA ATOLL *1975-96*

- area of high contamination
- nuclear test sites
- faults caused by nuclear tests

Mururoa atoll is a coral reef sitting on top of an extinct volcano that rises up from the ocean floor. France conducted 138 underground nuclear tests there from 1975 to 1996. The test shaft is drilled approximately one kilometre down into the rock. After the explosion, the top of the shaft is plugged with concrete to a depth of about 100 metres. The French government disputes assessments by independent experts that the atoll structure is seriously leaking radiation.

# 28 THE CALCULUS OF SECURITY

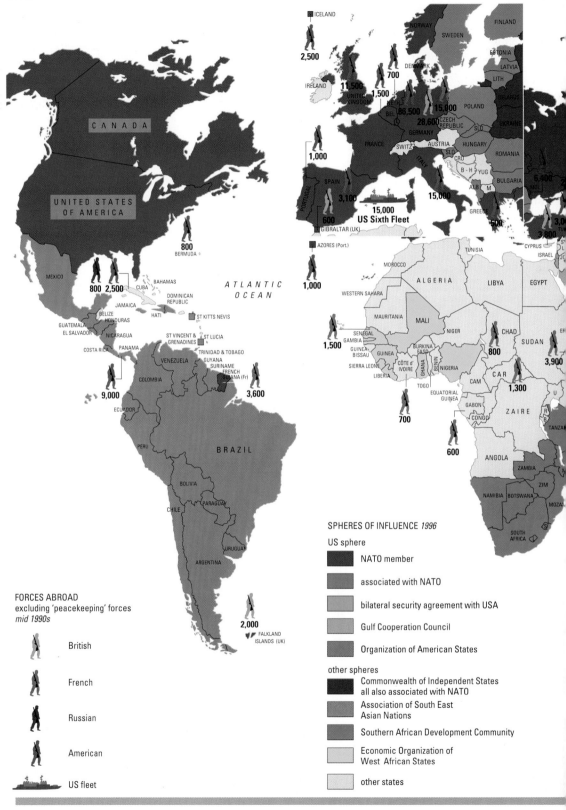

ICELAND
2,500

NORWAY SWEDEN FINLAND

ESTONIA
LATVIA
LITH
DENMARK 700
BELARUS

IRELAND
UNITED 11,500 1,500
KINGDOM
NETH
BEL 86,500 POLAND 15,000
CZECH 28,600
GERMANY REPUBLIC SLO UKRAINE
FRANCE SWITZ AUSTRIA HUNGARY
SLO ROMANIA
ITALY CRO
B - H YUG
1,000 BULGARIA 6,900
MOL
SPAIN ALB M
15,000 3,000
GREECE TUR
PORTUGAL 3,100 500 3,800
600 15,000
GIBRALTAR (UK) US Sixth Fleet CYPRUS

AZORES (Port.)
1,000

CANADA

UNITED STATES
OF AMERICA

800
BERMUDA

ATLANTIC
OCEAN

MEXICO

800 2,500 BAHAMAS
CUBA
JAMAICA DOMINICAN
REPUBLIC
BELIZE HAITI
GUATEMALA HONDURAS ST KITTS NEVIS
EL SALVADOR NICARAGUA
ST VINCENT & ST LUCIA
COSTA RICA PANAMA GRENADINES
TRINIDAD & TOBAGO
VENEZUELA GUYANA
SURINAME
COLOMBIA FRENCH
9,000 GUIANA (Fr) 3,600

ECUADOR

PERU BRAZIL

BOLIVIA

PARAGUAY
CHILE

URUGUAY

ARGENTINA

2,000
FALKLAND
ISLANDS (UK)

TUNISIA
MOROCCO
WESTERN SAHARA ISRAEL
ALGERIA LIBYA EGYPT

1,500 MAURITANIA MALI
NIGER CHAD SUDAN
SENEGAL 800
GAMBIA BURKINA
GUINEA- FASO ER
BISSAU GUINEA NIGERIA 3,900
SIERRA LEONE CÔTE d'
LIBERIA IVOIRE BENIN CAR
TOGO GHANA CAM 1,300 U
700 EQUATORIAL
GUINEA GABON
CONGO ZAIRE R
600 B TANZA

ANGOLA ZAMBIA

ZIM
NAMIBIA BOTSWANA MOZA

SOUTH S
AFRICA

## FORCES ABROAD
excluding 'peacekeeping' forces
*mid 1990s*

British

French

Russian

American

US fleet

## SPHERES OF INFLUENCE *1996*

US sphere

NATO member

associated with NATO

bilateral security agreement with USA

Gulf Cooperation Council

Organization of American States

other spheres

Commonwealth of Independent States
all also associated with NATO

Association of South East
Asian Nations

Southern African Development Community

Economic Organization of
West African States

other states

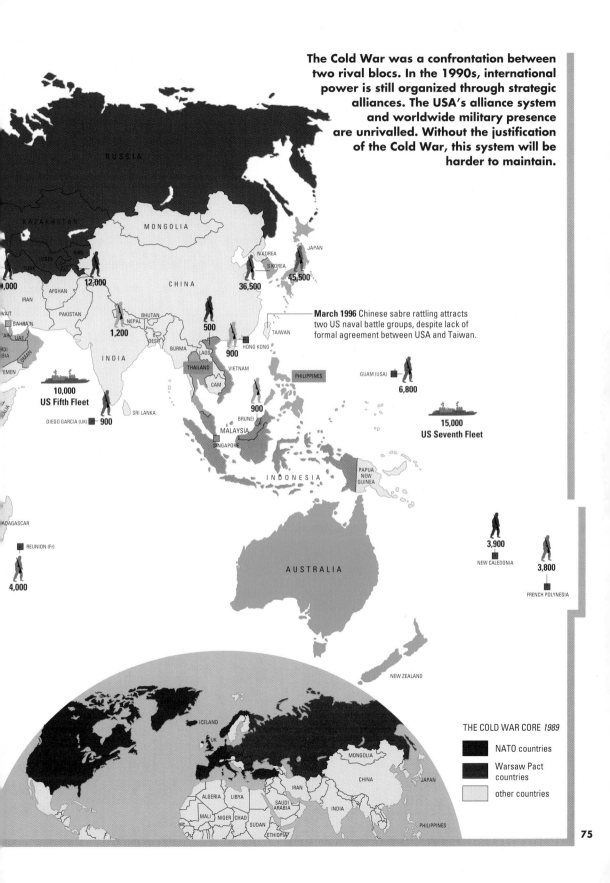

The Cold War was a confrontation between two rival blocs. In the 1990s, international power is still organized through strategic alliances. The USA's alliance system and worldwide military presence are unrivalled. Without the justification of the Cold War, this system will be harder to maintain.

RUSSIA

KAZAKHSTAN

MONGOLIA

N.KOREA

JAPAN

S.KOREA

45,500

,000

12,000

IRAN

AFGHAN

CHINA

36,500

**March 1996** Chinese sabre rattling attracts two US naval battle groups, despite lack of formal agreement between USA and Taiwan.

KUWAIT

BAHRAIN

ARY

UAE

PAKISTAN

BHUTAN

NEPAL

B.
DESH

500

TAIWAN

1,200

NDI
BIA

OMAN

INDIA

BURMA

LAOS

THAILAND

VIETNAM

900

HONG KONG

GUAM (USA)

EMEN

CAM

PHILIPPINES

6,800

10,000
US Fifth Fleet

SRI LANKA

900

15,000
US Seventh Fleet

DIEGO GARCIA (UK)    900

MALAYSIA

BRUNEI

SINGAPORE

INDONESIA

PAPUA
NEW
GUINEA

DAGASCAR

REUNION (Fr)

3,900

NEW CALEDONIA

3,800

4,000

AUSTRALIA

FRENCH POLYNESIA

NEW ZEALAND

THE COLD WAR CORE *1989*

ICELAND

UK

USSR

MONGOLIA

CHINA

JAPAN

NATO countries

Warsaw Pact
countries

other countries

ALGERIA

LIBYA

SAUDI
ARABIA

IRAN

INDIA

MALI

NIGER

CHAD

SUDAN

PHILIPPINES

ETHIOPIA

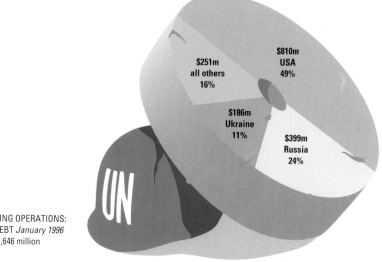

$251m
all others
16%

$810m
USA
49%

$186m
Ukraine
11%

$399m
Russia
24%

UN PEACEKEEPING OPERATIONS:
CUMULATIVE DEBT *January 1996*
Total debt US $1,646 million

# 29 IN THE SHADOW OF MASSACRE

Dan Smith *The State of War and Peace Atlas* 3rd edition Copyright © Myriad Editions Limited

**The UN spent nearly two billion US dollars overseeing Cambodia's transition to peace. The refugees returned and a new government was elected. But in 1995 and 1996 fighting continued in western areas.**

War started in Cambodia in 1970 as an offshoot of the Vietnam war. In 1975 the Communist Khmer Rouge was victorious. Massacres followed. Estimates of the death toll exceed three million – about 45 percent of the population.

In 1978 Vietnam invaded Cambodia and installed a new government. Prolonged guerrilla warfare began. Contacts between the warring parties were initiated in peace negotiations in December 1987. Vietnam finally withdrew in 1989. Renewed talks in 1990 finally produced the Paris Peace Agreement in October 1991. At that time the Phnom Penh government controlled about 90 percent of the country, the Khmer Rouge almost 10 percent and the other opposition groups very small areas.

A UN peacekeeping force went to Cambodia to bring back the refugees, disarm the fighters and arrange free and fair elections. It succeeded on two counts and failed on one – disarmament was patchy and the Khmer Rouge remained a well organized fighting force.

Even so, 360,000 refugees returned in a 14 month period. Elections were held in May 1993. The Khmer Rouge boycotted the elections, kept the war going, and killed 200 Cambodian citizens and UN observers. Despite this, in areas controlled by the Khmer Rouge, 80 percent of the population voted; nationally, the average turnout was 90 percent.

By 1993, at the end of the UN's two year operation, Cambodia had a democratically elected government and some foreign economic aid. The Khmer Rouge remained a formidable guerrilla force, although far short of its original strength, with some 10,000 fighters in 1993, dwindling to 5,000 by early 1996.

Cambodians face a further threat. Between six and ten million landmines litter 2,700 square kilometres of countryside. Only 13.5 square kilometres were cleared between 1992 and 1995, the first three years of the mine clearance programme. On the most optimistic assessment it will take at least 30 years to clear the rest.

## RETURN OF REFUGEES *1991-93*
Areas in which:

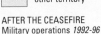

- more than 50,000 refugees settled
- 10,000-50,000 refugees settled
- 1,000-10,000 refugees settled
- less than 1,000 refugees settled
- other territory

## AFTER THE CEASEFIRE
Military operations *1992-96*

 major offensives by Khmer Rouge

major offensives by government forces

 UN force *main national contingent shown*

mine clearance programmes *1992-95*

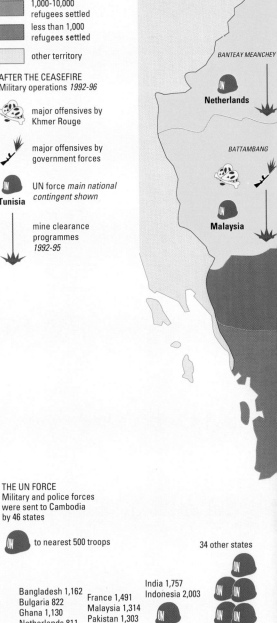

BANTEAY MEANCHEY

Netherlands

BATTAMBANG

Tunisia

Malaysia

## THE UN FORCE
Military and police forces were sent to Cambodia by 46 states

to nearest 500 troops

Bangladesh 1,162
Bulgaria 822
Ghana 1,130
Netherlands 811
Tunisia 912
Uruguay 940

Philippines 351

France 1,491
Malaysia 1,314
Pakistan 1,303

India 1,757
Indonesia 2,003

34 other states

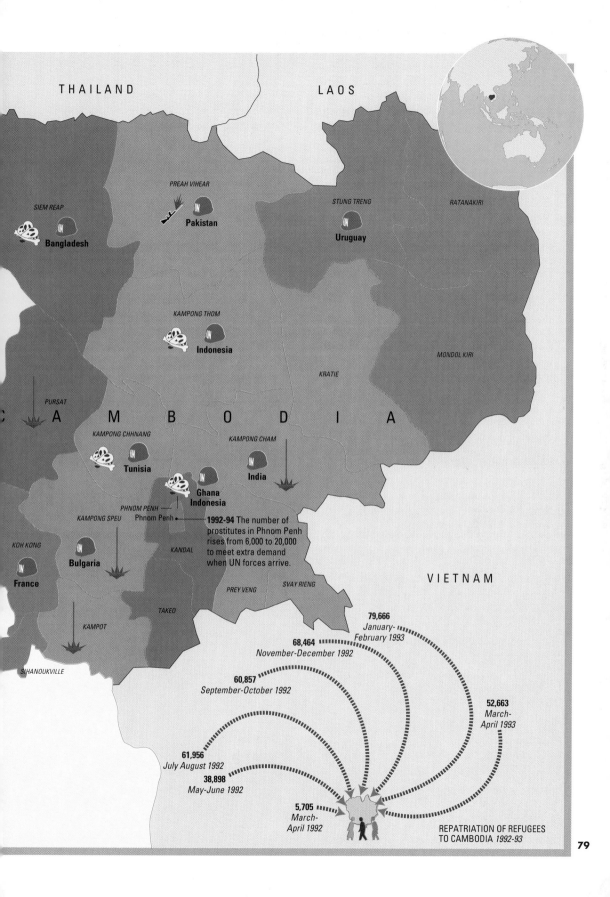

THAILAND

LAOS

SIEM REAP

Bangladesh

PREAH VIHEAR

Pakistan

STUNG TRENG

Uruguay

RATANAKIRI

KAMPONG THOM

Indonesia

KRATIE

MONDOL KIRI

PURSAT

C  A  M  B  O  D  I  A

KAMPONG CHHNANG

Tunisia

KAMPONG CHAM

India

Ghana
Indonesia

PHNOM PENH
Phnom Penh

KAMPONG SPEU

**1992-94** The number of
prostitutes in Phnom Penh
rises from 6,000 to 20,000
to meet extra demand
when UN forces arrive.

KOH KONG

KANDAL

Bulgaria

France

PREY VENG

SVAY RIENG

VIETNAM

TAKEO

KAMPOT

**79,666**
*January-
February 1993*

**68,464**
*November-December 1992*

SIHANOUKVILLE

**60,857**
*September-October 1992*

**52,663**
*March-
April 1993*

**61,956**
*July August 1992*

**38,898**
*May-June 1992*

**5,705**
*March-
April 1992*

REPATRIATION OF REFUGEES
TO CAMBODIA *1992-93*

# 30 THE ORANGE AND THE GREEN

Dan Smith *The State of War and Peace Atlas* 3rd edition Copyright © Myriad Editions Limited

**England's rulers first attempted to conquer Ireland in 1170. After eight centuries of intermittent, often brutal conflict, and a quarter of a century after the outbreak of the latest round of war, Ireland in the mid 1990s stood on the edge of peace.**

In 1993, Gerry Adams, leader of the republican party Sinn Fein, the political wing of the IRA, and John Hume, leader of the Social Democratic Labour Party, held secret talks. They paved the way for the Downing Street Declaration by the governments of Britain and Ireland. The Declaration offered negotiations with Sinn Fein, whilst assuring Protestant Loyalists that nothing would change except by majority vote. In August 1994, the IRA declared a ceasefire.

The ceasefire brought relief and a breathing space for negotiations but the issues in the conflict remained intractable. The Loyalist leaders still want union with Britain, even if Britain is not sure it wants union with Northern Ireland: British opinion polls in the 1990s indicated 70 percent approval of the idea of detaching Northern Ireland from Britain. The mostly Catholic Republican nationalists still want Irish unity, even though no recent Irish government has held to that objective. And while all parties agree that final decisions must be arrived at democratically, Irish nationalists want all Ireland to vote, whilst Loyalists say the decision is Northern Ireland's alone.

Negotiations were hampered by the British government's demand that the IRA give up its weapons first and talk later. This demand is rarely made – and even more rarely accepted – between opposite sides of an armed conflict. It reflected the British government's view that the IRA is not an army but a criminal organization.

In February 1996 the IRA responded to what it saw as a British tactic to delay proper negotiations by detonating a bomb in London's Docklands. Two people died and 43 were injured. In Northern Ireland the strongest force for peace appeared on the streets. One hundred and fifty thousand people, 10 percent of Northern Ireland's population, rallied in Belfast to demand that peace talks continue. The peace process, however, was hanging by a thread.

BELFAST — A DIVIDED CITY

- 80% Protestant area
- 80% Catholic area
- mixed community
- ——— 'Peace line': British army barrier between Protestants and Catholics
- ● IRA Battalion

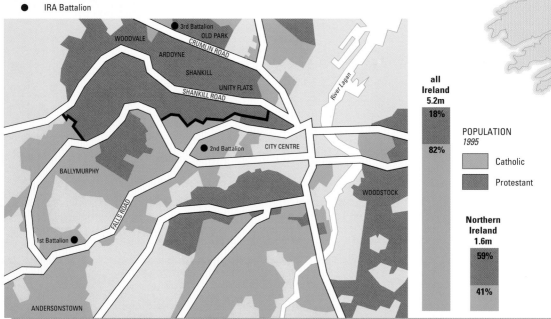

all Ireland 5.2m

18%

82%

POPULATION
*1995*

Catholic

Protestant

Northern Ireland 1.6m

59%

41%

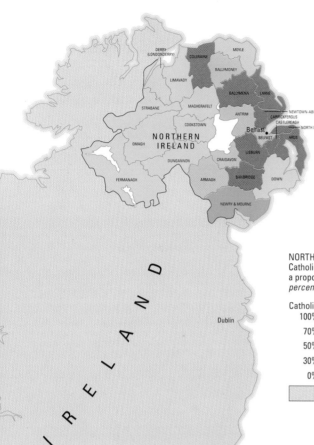

DERRY (LONDONDERRY)  MOYLE
COLERAINE
BALLYMONEY
LIMAVADY  BALLYMENA  LARNE
STRABANE  MAGHERAFELT
ANTRIM  NEWTOWN-ABBEY
COOKSTOWN  CARRICKFERGUS
CASTLEREAGH  NORTH DOWN
Belfast
NORTHERN  BELFAST  ARDS
IRELAND  OMAGH
LISBURN
DUNGANNON  CRAIGAVON
FERMANAGH  ARMAGH  BANBRIDGE  DOWN
NEWRY & MOURNE

I R E L A N D

Dublin

**NORTHERN IRELAND** *1991*
Catholics and Protestants as
a proportion of the population
*percentages*

| Catholic | | Protestant |
|---|---|---|
| 100% | | 0% |
| 70% | | 30% |
| 50% | | 50% |
| 30% | | 70% |
| 0% | | 100% |

Ireland

**1170** Norman invasion of Ireland.

**1250** Normans complete conquest
of Ireland.
**1297** Uprisings confine Normans to
small area around Dublin.

**1541** Henry VIII of England declares
himself ruler of all Ireland.

**1608** English and Scottish settlers
'planted' in Ulster (Northern Ireland).
**1649** Cromwell quashes uprisings.
**1690** King William III of England
wins decisive victory at Battle of the
Boyne.

**1700** Irish Catholics deprived of
property rights.
**1790s** Fifty thousand die in uprising
led by Protestant lawyer Wolfe Tone.

**1801** United Kingdom of Great
Britain and Ireland established.
**1840s-60s** Famines, uprisings.
**1885-1914** Attempts to grant Home
Rule in Ireland opposed by
Protestant businessmen,
landowners and army.

**1916** Easter Rising.
**1919** Irish Republican Army
launches new war of independence.
**1920** Britain partitions Ireland.

**1920 Partition**

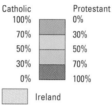

IRELAND

UNITED
KINGDOM

**1922** Independence war ends.
**1922-23** Civil war over partition.
**1925** Partition agreed: Ireland
independent; Northern Ireland
controlled by Protestant elite with
Catholics' civil rights severely
restricted.

**1949** UK parliament bars
reunification except with agreement
of a majority in Northern Ireland.

**1960s** Civil rights campaign
against anti Catholic discrimination
in Northern Ireland. Protestant
backlash.
**1969** Protestant march sparks
violence in Londonderry. British
army called in to restore order.

**1970** Provisional IRA launches
armed campaign.
**1971** Internment without trial
introduced; violence escalates.
**1973, 1985** Failed peace initiatives.
**1993** New peace initiative.
**1994** Ceasefire
**1996** Ceasefire broken.

**THE DEATH TOLL**
War deaths in Northern Ireland *1969-93*
*total numbers and division between
deaths of civilians and security forces*
percentages

civilian deaths

security forces' deaths

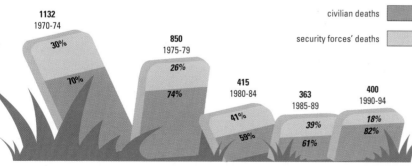

**1132**
1970-74
30%
70%

**850**
1975-79
26%
74%

**415**
1980-84
41%
59%

**363**
1985-89
39%
61%

**400**
1990-94
18%
82%

# 31 LANDS OF GOOD HOPE

Dan Smith *The State of War and Peace Atlas* 3rd edition Copyright © Myriad Editions Limited

**Apartheid was one of the most cruel and unjust political systems ever devised. Though it continues to cast a shadow of violence over South Africa, its end has brought hope to the country, the region and further afield.**

On 11 February 1990, an international television audience saw Nelson Mandela emerge from more than 25 years in prison. By the end of 1993, when he and President de Klerk shared the Nobel Peace Prize, they had agreed an interim constitution for South Africa. The country's first free and fair elections were held in April 1994. Mandela was elected President.

Political tension remained widespread and rivalry between the African National Congress and the Inkatha 'Freedom' Party led to over 1,000 deaths in less than two years. In an attempt to defuse the violence, the new government trained several hundred peace negotiators and set up local commissions for peace and reconciliation throughout the country.

The beginning of change in South Africa, even before the demise of apartheid, helped to bring peace and independence to Namibia. It also helped the peace efforts in Angola and Mozambique, where insurgent forces could no longer depend on the support of South Africa's apartheid regime. In Mozambique, the October 1992 peace agreement ended 16 years of vicious warfare and led to elections in 1994. The government won, despite receiving less than half the votes, and the former armed insurgents accepted the result.

In Angola, the process has been tougher. A 1991 ceasefire led to elections in 1992 but war resumed when the UNITA opposition rejected the result. A new peace agreement was signed in November 1994. Ceasefire violations continued throughout 1995 and into 1996.

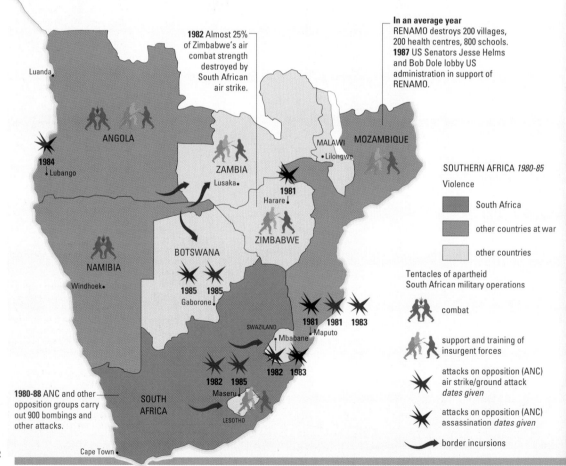

**1982** Almost 25% of Zimbabwe's air combat strength destroyed by South African air strike.

**In an average year**
RENAMO destroys 200 villages, 200 health centres, 800 schools.
**1987** US Senators Jesse Helms and Bob Dole lobby US administration in support of RENAMO.

Luanda

ANGOLA

**1984**
Lubango

ZAMBIA
Lusaka

MALAWI
Lilongwe

MOZAMBIQUE

**1981**
Harare

ZIMBABWE

BOTSWANA

NAMIBIA
Windhoek

**1985    1985**
Gaborone

SWAZILAND
Mbabane

**1981  1981   1983**
Maputo

**1982  1983**

**1982   1985**
Maseru

SOUTH AFRICA

LESOTHO

**1980-88** ANC and other opposition groups carry out 900 bombings and other attacks.

Cape Town

SOUTHERN AFRICA *1980-85*

Violence

South Africa

other countries at war

other countries

Tentacles of apartheid
South African military operations

combat

support and training of insurgent forces

attacks on opposition (ANC) air strike/ground attack *dates given*

attacks on opposition (ANC) assassination *dates given*

border incursions

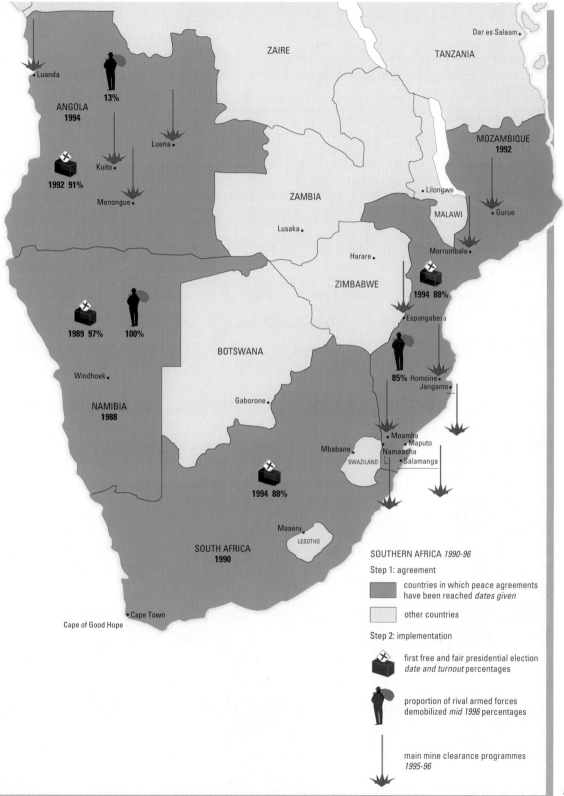

ZAIRE

TANZANIA

Dar es Salaam •

• Luanda

ANGOLA
**1994**

13%

Luena •

Kuito •

**1992 91%**

Menongue •

MOZAMBIQUE
**1992**

• Lilongwe

MALAWI

• Gurue

Morrumbala •

ZAMBIA

Lusaka •

Harare •

ZIMBABWE

**1994 88%**

Espungabera •

**1989 97%**    100%

BOTSWANA

Windhoek •

NAMIBIA
**1988**

Gaborone •

85% Homoine •
Jangamo •

• Moamba
• Maputo
Namaacha
• Salamanga

Mbabane •

SWAZILAND

**1994 88%**

Maseru •

LESOTHO

SOUTH AFRICA
**1990**

• Cape Town

Cape of Good Hope

SOUTHERN AFRICA *1990-96*

Step 1: agreement

countries in which peace agreements
have been reached *dates given*

other countries

Step 2: implementation

first free and fair presidential election
*date and turnout* percentages

proportion of rival armed forces
demobilized *mid 1996* percentages

main mine clearance programmes
*1995-96*

83

# 32 KEEPING PEACE

**In the first six years after the end of the Cold War, the UN put more military operations into conflict areas than it did in the previous 40 years. Widely referred to as peacekeeping forces, they sometimes fulfil that aim.**

The United Nations' peacekeeping forces aim to help two parties, who are used to war but want peace, to break old habits. UN forces monitor ceasefires, separate rivals, and sort out contentious issues. They are equipped with light weapons only and have strict instructions to fire only when fired on and only as a last resort.

At the beginning of the 1990s, several conflicts around the world were settled and demand for the 'Blue Helmets' increased. But in Somalia and, especially, in Bosnia-Herzegovina, the UN peacekeepers ran into serious trouble. The credibility of all UN operations was threatened as a result. But in neither country was there any peace to keep. If there was a role for external military intervention, it was not for lightly armed peacekeepers. Elsewhere, they have continued to be of use.

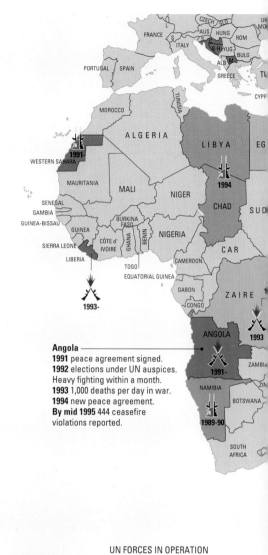

**Angola**
**1991** peace agreement signed.
**1992** elections under UN auspices. Heavy fighting within a month.
**1993** 1,000 deaths per day in war.
**1994** new peace agreement.
**By mid 1995** 444 ceasefire violations reported.

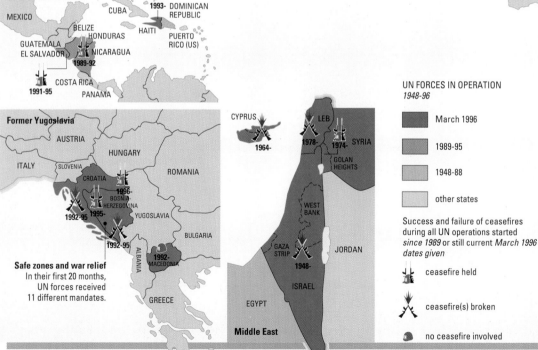

**Central America**

**1993-** DOMINICAN REPUBLIC

**Former Yugoslavia**

**Safe zones and war relief**
In their first 20 months, UN forces received 11 different mandates.

**Middle East**

**UN FORCES IN OPERATION**
*1948-96*

March 1996

1989-95

1948-88

other states

Success and failure of ceasefires during all UN operations started *since 1989* or still current *March 1996* dates given

⚔ ceasefire held

⚔ ceasefire(s) broken

⚔ no ceasefire involved

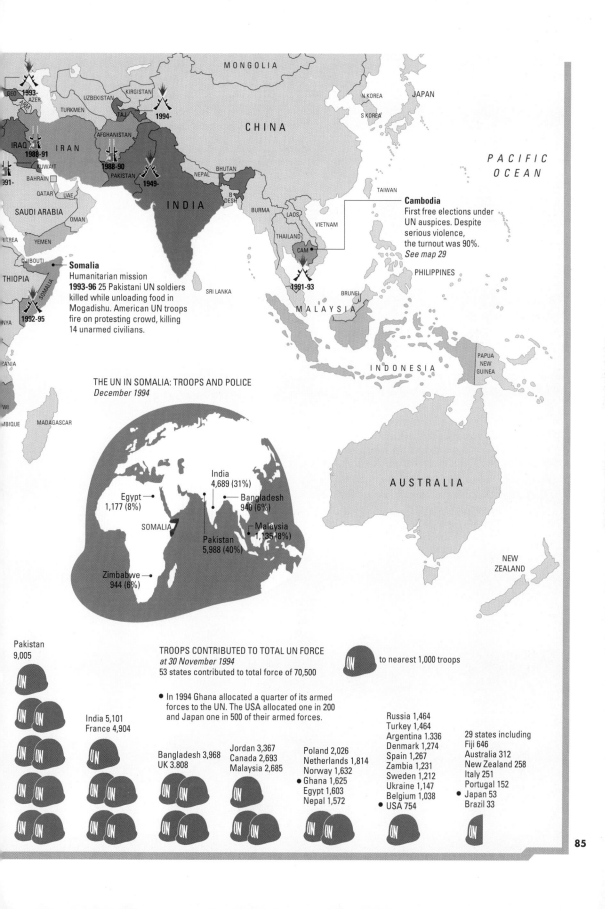

MONGOLIA

CHINA

JAPAN

N KOREA

S KOREA

*PACIFIC OCEAN*

UZBEKISTAN

KIRGISTAN

TURKMEN

TAJ.

**1994-**

**GEO 1993-**
AZER

AFGHANISTAN

IRAQ
**1988-91**

IRAN

KUWAIT

BAHRAIN

91-

QATAR   UAE

SAUDI ARABIA

OMAN

YEMEN

ERITREA

DJIBOUTI

THIOPIA

PAKISTAN
**1988-90**

**1949-**

NEPAL   BHUTAN

B
DESH

INDIA

BURMA

LAOS

VIETNAM

THAILAND

CAM

**1991-93**

TAIWAN

PHILIPPINES

BRUNEI

MALAYSIA

INDONESIA

PAPUA
NEW
GUINEA

**Cambodia**
First free elections under
UN auspices. Despite
serious violence,
the turnout was 90%.
*See map 29*

**Somalia**
Humanitarian mission
**1993-96** 25 Pakistani UN soldiers
killed while unloading food in
Mogadishu. American UN troops
fire on protesting crowd, killing
14 unarmed civilians.

SRI LANKA

**1992-95**

NYA

ZANIA

WI

MBIQUE

MADAGASCAR

AUSTRALIA

NEW
ZEALAND

THE UN IN SOMALIA: TROOPS AND POLICE
*December 1994*

India
4,689 (31%)

Egypt
1,177 (8%)

Bangladesh
940 (6%)

SOMALIA

Malaysia
1,135 (8%)

Pakistan
5,988 (40%)

Zimbabwe
944 (6%)

Pakistan
9,005

TROOPS CONTRIBUTED TO TOTAL UN FORCE
*at 30 November 1994*
53 states contributed to total force of 70,500

to nearest 1,000 troops

• In 1994 Ghana allocated a quarter of its armed
forces to the UN. The USA allocated one in 200
and Japan one in 500 of their armed forces.

India 5,101
France 4,904

Bangladesh 3,968
UK 3.808

Jordan 3,367
Canada 2,693
Malaysia 2,685

Poland 2,026
Netherlands 1,814
Norway 1,632
• Ghana 1,625
Egypt 1,603
Nepal 1,572

Russia 1,464
Turkey 1,464
Argentina 1.336
Denmark 1,274
Spain 1,267
Zambia 1,231
Sweden 1,212
Ukraine 1,147
Belgium 1,038
• USA 754

29 states including
Fiji 646
Australia 312
New Zealand 258
Italy 251
Portugal 152
• Japan 53
Brazil 33

# 33 FORCING PEACE

**During the 1990s, more than 60 states have used forces for peacekeeping operations outside the UN framework – for mixed reasons and with mixed results.**

It is sometimes easier to keep the peace – and occasionally it is possible to enforce it – by using forces that are allowed to use more firepower more freely than UN forces. Following this principle, a NATO force was deployed to support the 1995 peace agreement in Bosnia-Herzegovina – after the UN peacekeeping operation had been discredited as passive and futile.

At other times, 'peacekeeping' is a cover for a traditional strategic power play. Russia's regional peacekeeping operations have stopped the fighting in Moldova and Georgia, but the issues in conflict have not been resolved and refugees have not returned. In Tajikistan, Russia's aim was to support the government and secure the border with Afghanistan. This was achieved, but not peace.

Both the 1992 US intervention in Somalia and the 1994 French action in Rwanda were justified on humanitarian grounds. But neither operation had a discernible effect on the war or the scale of the human tragedies. In Somalia, the US handed command over to the UN, which accordingly took the blame for everything that went wrong. In Rwanda, French forces established a safe area for refugees only to abandon it two months later.

In March 1995, three South Pacific island states, backed by Australia and New Zealand, put a force into Bougainville to gain time for peace negotiations. When there was no breakthrough in the talks a month later, the force pulled out; fighting resumed within twenty four hours.

The 1994 US action in Haiti did achieve its aims. It levered out the military dictatorship and returned the democratically elected President Jean-Bertrand Aristide to office. Six months later, command was transferred to the UN.

*see also Map 32*

**Haiti** *1994-95*
**21,000 troops from USA**
**1,000 from 12 other states**

**Liberia** *1990-*
**8,000 troops from Nigeria**
**2,000 from 7 other states**

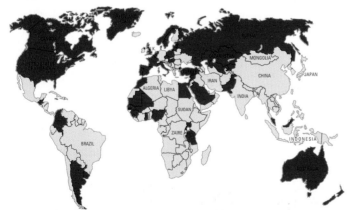

PEACE ENFORCING
except UN operations
*1996*

- states sending peace enforcement troops abroad
- other countries

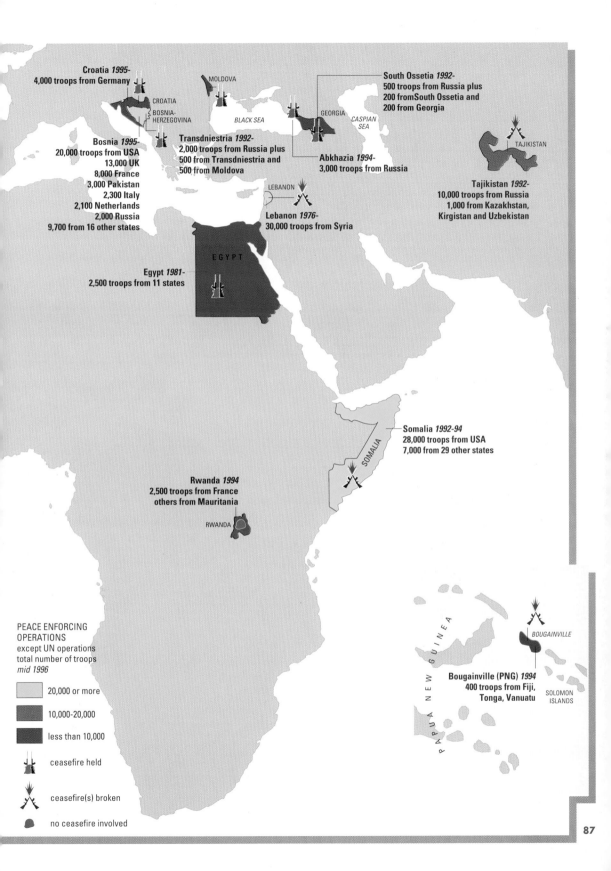

Croatia *1995-*
4,000 troops from Germany

CROATIA

BOSNIA-
HERZEGOVINA

MOLDOVA

*BLACK SEA*

GEORGIA

*CASPIAN
SEA*

South Ossetia *1992-*
500 troops from Russia plus
200 fromSouth Ossetia and
200 from Georgia

TAJIKISTAN

Bosnia *1995-*
20,000 troops from USA
13,000 UK
8,000 France
3,000 Pakistan
2,300 Italy
2,100 Netherlands
2,000 Russia
9,700 from 16 other states

Transdniestria *1992-*
2,000 troops from Russia plus
500 from Transdniestria and
500 from Moldova

Abkhazia *1994-*
3,000 troops from Russia

Tajikistan *1992-*
10,000 troops from Russia
1,000 from Kazakhstan,
Kirgistan and Uzbekistan

LEBANON

Lebanon *1976-*
30,000 troops from Syria

EGYPT

Egypt *1981-*
2,500 troops from 11 states

Somalia *1992-94*
28,000 troops from USA
7,000 from 29 other states

SOMALIA

Rwanda *1994*
2,500 troops from France
others from Mauritania

RWANDA

PAPUA NEW GUINEA

BOUGAINVILLE

Bougainville (PNG) *1994*
400 troops from Fiji,
Tonga, Vanuatu

SOLOMON
ISLANDS

PEACE ENFORCING
OPERATIONS
except UN operations
total number of troops
*mid 1996*

20,000 or more

10,000-20,000

less than 10,000

ceasefire held

ceasefire(s) broken

no ceasefire involved

THE PEACEMAKERS *1990s*
Home bases of independent conflict resolution
groups and number of active conflict resolution
projects.

| 1 | 2 | 4 | 7 |
|---|---|---|---|
| Italy, Spain Switzerland | Costa Rica | Ethiopia | Kenya, Netherland Sweden, UK |

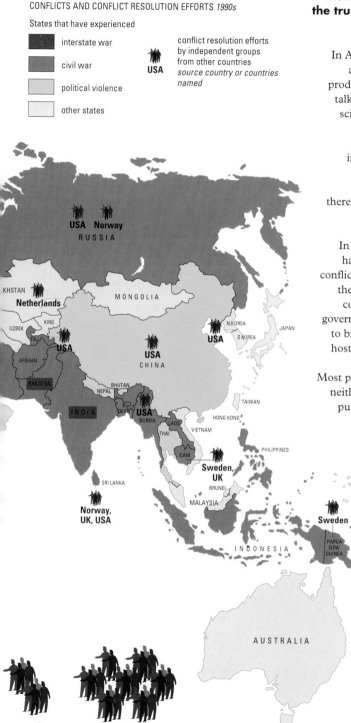

CONFLICTS AND CONFLICT RESOLUTION EFFORTS *1990s*

States that have experienced

- interstate war
- civil war
- political violence
- other states

conflict resolution efforts by independent groups from other countries
**USA** *source country or countries named*

USA  Norway
RUSSIA

KHSTAN
**Netherlands**

UZBEK    KIRG

MONGOLIA

**USA**

AFGHAN

**USA**
CHINA

PAKISTAN

BHUTAN
NEPAL

B.
**DESH  USA**
BURMA

INDIA

SRI LANKA

LAOS
THAI    VIETNAM

CAM

**Sweden,
UK**

N.KOREA

**USA**  S KOREA

JAPAN

TAIWAN

HONG KONG

PHILIPPINES

BRUNEI

MALAYSIA

**Norway,
UK, USA**

INDONESIA

**Sweden**

PAPUA
NEW
GUINEA

AUSTRALIA

**8
Norway**

**26
USA**

NEW ZEALAND

**Independent organizations are sometimes more able than any government to gain the trust of contending parties. This can be a first step to resolving conflict.**

In August 1993, the world heard about a peace agreement between Israel and the PLO, the product of an Oslo 'back channel'. Confidential talks had been arranged by a Norwegian social science research institute. From time to time, more news breaks about quiet diplomacy, informal contacts, mediation by private individuals or organizations. Little is known about these processes until and unless they succeed. For every one that does succeed, there are several that do not. But even these can lay the groundwork for future efforts.

In the 1990s, an increasing number of people have been trained in the skills of negotiation, conflict resolution and reconciliation. They apply their skills at every level, from disputes within communities to negotiations between hostile governments trying to prevent violence. They try to bring an end to hostilities and to ensure that hostilities, once ended, do not break out again.

Most people involved in conflict resolution efforts neither expect nor receive very much by way of public thanks. Their gratification comes from knowing that, usually in a small way and very occasionally in a spectacular way, they have done something to change the world for the better.

# TABLE OF WARS 1990-95

| | 1<br>type of war | 2<br>site of war | 3<br>adversaries<br>interstate war only |
|---|---|---|---|
| Afghanistan | civil war | general | – |
| Algeria | civil war | general | – |
| Angola | civil war | general | – |
| | regional civil war | Cabinda enclave | – |
| Armenia | interstate war | Nagorno Karabakh | Azerbaijan |
| Azerbaijan | interstate war | Nagorno Karabakh | Armenia |
| Bangladesh | regional civil war | Chittagong | – |
| Bosnia-Herzegovina | civil war | general | – |
| Burma | regional civil war | Kachin | – |
| | regional civil war | Shan | – |
| | regional civil war | Karen | – |
| | civil war | general | – |
| | regional civil war | Arakan | – |
| | regional civil war | Kaya | – |
| Burundi | civil war | general | – |
| Cambodia | civil war | general | – |
| Chad | civil war | general | – |
| Colombia | civil war | general | – |
| Congo | civil war | general | |
| Croatia | civil and interstate war | Slavonia /Krajina | Serbia |
| | regional civil war | Western Slavonia / Krajina | – |
| Djibouti | regional civil war | Afar | – |
| Ecuador | interstate war | border region | Peru |
| Egypt | civil war | general | – |
| El Salvador | civil war | general | – |
| Eritrea | war of independence | Eritrea | Ethiopia |
| Ethiopia | against war of independence | Eritrea | Eritrea |
| | civil war | general | – |
| France | interstate war | Kuwait/ Iraq | Iraq |
| Georgia | regional civil war | western region | – |
| | regional civil war | South Ossetia | – |
| | regional civil war | Abkhazia | – |
| Ghana | regional civil war | northern regions | – |
| Guatemala | civil war | general | – |
| Haiti | civil war | general | – |
| India | interstate war | Kashmir | Pakistan |
| | regional civil war | Kashmir | – |
| | regional civil war | Andhra Pradesh | – |
| | regional civil war | Punjab | – |
| | regional civil war | Assam | – |
| Indonesia | regional civil war | Irian Jaya | – |
| | regional civil war | East Timor | – |
| | regional civil war | Sumatra | – |

| 4 war began | 5 combat status 31 December 1995 | |
|---|---|---|
| 1978 | continuing | Afghanistan |
| 1992 | continuing | Algeria |
| 1975 | continuing | Angola |
| 1978 | continuing | |
| 1990 | suspended by agreement 1994 | Armenia |
| 1990 | suspended by agreement 1994 | Azerbaijan |
| 1973 | suspended by agreement 1992 | Bangladesh |
| 1992 | suspended by agreement 1995 | Bosnia-Herzegovina |
| 1948 | suspended by agreement 1994 | Burma |
| 1948 | continuing | |
| 1949 | continuing | |
| 1991 | suspended by decisive break in action 1992 | |
| 1992 | suspended by agreement 1994 | |
| 1992 | continuing | |
| 1988 | continuing | Burundi |
| 1970 | continuing | Cambodia |
| 1965 | continuing | Chad |
| 1986 | continuing | Colombia |
| 1993 | suspended by agreement 1994 | Congo |
| 1991 | suspended by agreement 1992 | Croatia |
| 1995 | suspended by agreement 1995 | |
| 1991 | continuing | Djibouti |
| 1995 | suspended by agreement 1995 | Ecuador |
| 1992 | continuing | Egypt |
| 1979 | suspended by agreement 1991 | El Salvador |
| 1962 | suspended by agreement 1991 | Eritrea |
| 1962 | suspended by agreement 1991 | Ethiopia |
| 1974 | suspended by agreement 1991 | |
| 1991 | suspended by agreement 1991 | France |
| 1991 | suspended by decisive break in action 1993 | Georgia |
| 1991 | suspended by agreement 1992 | |
| 1992 | suspended by agreement 1993 | |
| 1994 | suspended by decisive break in action 1995 | Ghana |
| 1968 | continuing | Guatemala |
| 1991 | suspended by decisive break in action 1991 | Haiti |
| 1982 | suspended by decisive break in action 1992 | India |
| 1990 | continuing | |
| 1969 | continuing | |
| 1981 | suspended by decisive break in action 1993 | |
| 1987 | continuing | |
| 1963 | continuing | Indonesia |
| 1975 | continuing | |
| 1989 | suspended by decisive break in action 1994 | |

# TABLE OF WARS 1990-95

| | 1<br>type of war | 2<br>site of war | 3<br>adversaries<br>interstate war only |
|---|---|---|---|
| Iran | civil war | general | – |
| | regional civil war | northwestern Kurdish regions | – |
| Iraq | regional civil war | northern regions/Kurdistan | – |
| | interstate war | Iraq /Kuwait | Kuw, Fr, S. Arabia, Syria, UK, |
| | regional civil war | southern Shia regions | – |
| Israel | civil war | general incl. occupied territories | – |
| Kurdistan see Map 13 | regional civil war | Turkish border regions | – |
| | civil war | general | – |
| Kuwait | interstate war | Kuwait / Iraq | Iraq |
| Laos | civil war | general | – |
| Lebanon | general, then regional civil war | southern zone, from 1990 | – |
| Liberia | civil war | general | – |
| Libya | civil war | general | – |
| Mali | regional civil war | northern Tuareg regions | – |
| Mauritania | interstate war | border regions | Senegal |
| Mexico | regional civil war | Chiapas | – |
| Moldova | regional civil war | Dniestr Republic | – |
| Morocco | against war of independence | Western Sahara | Polisario Front |
| Mozambique | civil war | general | – |
| Nicaragua | civil war | general | – |
| Niger | regional civil war | northern Tuareg regions | – |
| | regional civil war | eastern region | – |
| Pakistan | interstate war | Kashmir | India |
| | regional civil war | Karachi/Sind | – |
| Papua New Guinea | regional civil war | Bougainville | – |
| Peru | civil war | general | – |
| | interstate war | border region | Ecuador |
| Philippines | civil war | general | – |
| | regional civil war | Mindanao | – |
| Russia | regional civil war | North Ossetia/Ingushetia | – |
| | regional civil war | Moscow | – |
| | regional civil war | Chechnya | – |
| Rwanda | civil war | general | – |
| Saudi Arabia | interstate war | Kuwait / Iraq | Iraq |
| Senegal | interstate war | border regions | Mauritania |
| | regional civil war | Casamance region | – |
| Sierra Leone | civil war | general | – |
| Slovenia | interstate war | Slovenia | Yugoslavia |
| Somalia | civil war | general | – |
| Somaliland see Map 19 | civil war | general | – |
| South Africa | civil war | general | – |
| Spain | regional civil war | Basque region | – |

| 4<br>war began | 5<br>combat status<br>31 December 1995 | |
|---|---|---|
| 1978 | suspended by decisive break in action 1993 | Iran |
| 1979 | suspended by decisive break in action 1995 | |
| 1974 | continuing | Iraq |
| 1990 | suspended by agreement 1991 | |
| 1991 | continuing | |
| 1948 | continuing | Israel |
| 1991 | continuing | see Map 13 *Kurdistan* |
| 1993 | continuing | |
| 1990 | suspended by agreement 1991 | Kuwait |
| 1975 | suspended by decisive break in action 1990 | Laos |
| 1975 | continuing | Lebanon |
| 1989 | continuing | Liberia |
| 1995 | continuing | Libya |
| 1990 | suspended by agreement 1995 | Mali |
| 1989 | suspended by agreement 1991 | Mauritania |
| 1994 | suspended by agreement 1995 | Mexico |
| 1991 | suspended by agreement 1992 | Moldova |
| 1975 | suspended by decisive break in action 1991 | Morocco |
| 1976 | suspended by agreement 1992 | Mozambique |
| 1970 | suspended by agreement 1990 | Nicaragua |
| 1991 | continuing | Niger |
| 1994 | continuing | |
| 1982 | suspended by decisive break in action 1992 | Pakistan |
| 1992 | continuing | |
| 1988 | continuing | Papua New Guinea |
| 1980 | continuing | Peru |
| 1995 | suspended by agreement 1995 | |
| 1969 | continuing | Philippines |
| 1974 | continuing | |
| 1992 | suspended by decisive break in action 1992 | Russia |
| 1993 | suspended by decisive break in action 1993 | |
| 1994 | continuing | |
| 1990 | suspended by decisive break in action 1995 | Rwanda |
| 1991 | suspended by agreement 1991 | Saudi Arabia |
| 1989 | suspended by agreement 1991 | Senegal |
| 1990 | continuing | |
| 1991 | continuing | Sierra Leone |
| 1991 | suspended by agreement 1991 | Slovenia |
| 1977 | continuing | Somalia |
| 1991 | suspended by decisive break in action 1995 | see Map 19 *Somaliland* |
| 1984 | suspended by agreement 1994 | South Africa |
| 1968 | suspended by decisive break in action 1992 | Spain |

# TABLE OF WARS 1990-95

| | 1<br>**type of war** | 2<br>**site of war** | 3<br>**adversaries**<br>interstate war only |
|---|---|---|---|
| Sri Lanka | regional civil war | Tamil areas/ northeast | – |
| | civil war | general | – |
| Sudan | regional civil war | southern regions | – |
| | regional civil war | Beja | – |
| Suriname | civil war | general | – |
| Syria | interstate war | Kuwait/Iraq | Iraq |
| Tajikistan | civil war | general | – |
| Togo | civil war | general | – |
| Trinidad and Tobago | civil war | general | – |
| Turkey | regional civil war | SE Kurdish region/northern Iraq | – |
| | regional civil war | western region | – |
| Uganda | regional civil war | northern region | – |
| | regional civil war | central region | – |
| | regional civil war | southeastern region | – |
| United Kingdom | regional civil war | Northern Ireland | – |
| | interstate war | Kuwait/Iraq | Iraq |
| United States of America | interstate war | Kuwait/Iraq | Iraq |
| Venezuela | civil war | general | – |
| Western Sahara | war of independence | Western Sahara | Morocco |
| Yemen | civil war | general | – |
| Yugoslavia | interstate war | Slovenia | Slovenia |
| | interstate war | Croatia | Croatia |

| 4<br>war began | 5<br>combat status<br>31 December 1995 | |
| --- | --- | --- |
| 1977 | continuing | Sri Lanka |
| 1983 | suspended by decisive break in action 1990 | |
| 1955 | continuing | Sudan |
| 1994 | suspended by decisive break in action 1995 | |
| 1986 | suspended by agreement 1992 | Suriname |
| 1991 | suspended by agreement 1991 | Syria |
| 1992 | continuing | Tajikistan |
| 1991 | suspended by decisive break in action 1991 | Togo |
| 1990 | suspended by decisive break in action 1990 | Trinidad and Tobago |
| 1977 | continuing | Turkey |
| 1991 | suspended by decisive break in action 1992 | |
| 1986 | continuing | Uganda |
| 1994 | suspended by decisive break in action 1995 | |
| 1994 | suspended by decisive break in action 1995 | |
| 1969 | suspended by agreement 1994 | United Kingdom |
| 1991 | suspended by agreement 1991 | |
| 1991 | suspended by agreement 1991 | United States of America |
| 1992 | suspended by decisive break in action 1992 | Venezuela |
| 1975 | suspended by decisive break in action 1991 | Western Sahara |
| 1994 | suspended by agreement 1994 | Yemen |
| 1991 | suspended by agreement 1991 | Yugoslavia |
| 1991 | suspended by agreement 1992 | |

# NOTES

## 2 CONFLICTS OF INTEREST

There is no single cause of any war and there is no single social, economic or political element that stands out as the primary cause of contemporary armed conflict. But among the cluster of social facts that are repeatedly found in the background to conflict, poverty is one of the most obvious and the most easily identifiable.

Definitions of poverty are sometimes misleading. Not all communities that lack the modern amenities of the rich world should be regarded as impoverished; there are austere life styles that are perfectly sustainable. Data can also mislead. The modern obsession with national statistics and annual reporting misses much of the reality of lives in communities where not everything can be bought, sold and reduced to a statistic. And the process of reporting the statistics can be unreliable in its own terms, when information is incomplete or out of date. These problems are compounded when dealing, as this map does, with simple national averages: rich countries have poor people and poor countries have rich people, but national averages do not let one see the regional, gender and class variations.

The connections between poverty and conflict are also complex. Not every person living in poverty either turns to crime or joins the guerrillas in the mountains. One needs to look more closely at the specific conditions to see how politics (**3 Regimes and Rights**) and ethnicity (**4 Blood and Soil**) affect choices and loyalties.

The data on national wealth in this map come from the World Bank. The data on debt come from the World Bank, the OECD and various national governments. The intricacies of data on war are discussed in the note to the **Table of Wars 1990-95**. Much of the research for this map was by Wenche Hauge.

## 3 REGIMES AND RIGHTS

Two thirds of armed conflicts in the 1990s involve states that sanction the killing of political opponents and those whom they regard as socially undesirable. Of these states, almost 80 percent were involved in armed conflict in the 1990s.

Data and definitions on human rights abuse are often uncertain. The category of extrajudicial execution excludes war deaths but includes non legal killings by state authorities in connection with a war – arbitrary execution of suspected collaborators, for example – along with killings for other political and social reasons, including those carried out by off duty police officers, such as in the slaughter of street children in Brazil and Guatemala.

Torture also raises problems of definition. The UN definition includes any act by or at the instigation of a public official, which intentionally inflicts severe pain or suffering, whether physical or mental, for purposes such as intimidation of the victim or of others, punishment or obtaining a confession. This is evidently a very inclusive definition. Under it, depending on the meaning of 'severe', numerous police forces should be indicted for torture. This map reserves the term for egregious mistreatment that is deliberately designed to extort information or a confession, or which is part of a judicially approved punishment such as caning or flogging. It includes less serious cases, policies or practices under the heading of mistreatment. Restricting the definition of torture in this way reflects the gradations of pain and brutality that people normally have in mind when using the term. The thin line between torture and mistreatment depends on both the intention and the specific nature of the act.

Arbitrary arrest and detention means holding people in detention in a way that does not correspond to national law or to international standards. I have included the arbitrary treatment of asylum seekers and immigrants under this heading, and within that have included arbitrary expulsion as well as detention, since it is equally much a denial of basic freedom.

It is worth noting the emphasis in the map key on reports. Knowledge of human rights abuses depends on people reporting those abuses to international agencies. The outstanding one is Amnesty International, from whose reports most of the data for this map were taken. The intricacies of data on war are discussed in the note to the **Table of Wars 1990-95**. Much of the research for this map was by Wenche Hauge.

## 4 BLOOD AND SOIL

It was once generally assumed that the modern, global economy would obliterate ethnic differences and national sentiment. In the mid 1990s there is little support for that view. Ethnic diversity alone is not the cause of conflict, and many ethnically diverse societies are peaceful, but ethnic and nationalist conflicts are an important part of world politics today.

Ethnic and national identity constantly elude definition. Contemplating the insurmountable problem of a useful and universally applicable definition of what makes a nation, the eminent historian Hugh Seton-Watson remarked that, 'All I can find to say is that a nation exists when a significant number of people in a community consider themselves to form a nation, or behave as if they formed one.'

Nation building over the past two centuries has sometimes involved a relatively benign fusing of disparate ethnic identities to create a new national identity. More often, it has meant destroying the identity of weaker ethnic groups and basing national identity on the strongest group. Ethnic identity is destroyed in schools, as children are taught a new language and punished if they speak the language they have grown up with. It is destroyed when the names for people and places are banned: Bulgaria has banned ethnic Turkish names, for example, and Turkey has banned ethnic Kurdish names. It is destroyed through mass conscription, taking peasant boys into the national army and drumming old ethnic habits out of them. Ethnic identity is destroyed economically, when land is given to outsiders, or left behind in the search for work. And it is destroyed through warfare and the physical destruction of villages and expulsion of their inhabitants. And yet through all this, ethnic identity has proved to be extremely resilient. The effort to destroy it is often what creates a new nationalist movement.

Statistics based on ethnic categories simplify a complex and changing reality, creating massive uncertainties in data. Even when census authorities do not cook the books, unconscious biases may enter a population census. It is often hard to spot these biases and, when spotted, nonetheless impossible to correct them. Definitions and counting procedures vary between countries. Some governments do not count ethnic minorities at all. There are good and bad reasons for this. One reason is in order to obliterate minorities from the official mind — a process that usually has a more or less violent practical expression as well. Another quite different reason is in order to assert that whatever the people's colour, creed or origin, everyone has equal rights. It is therefore difficult to know how to treat 'melting pot' societies such as Australia, Canada and, most strikingly, the USA, in which some ethnic differences are no longer counted while others are included. In general, I have taken a deep breath and followed official statistics, even when they exclude non nationals, that is, resident foreigners. This produces an inaccurate picture of some countries, especially the Arab Gulf states, with their large populations of migrant labour. The intricacies of data on war are discussed in the note to the **Table of Wars 1990-95**.

## 5 UNLICENSED TERROR

Most people feel a special repugnance when they think of terrorism. It seems to be an unfair form of war, often deliberately aimed at innocent bystanders. But what is it that identifies bombs on Baghdad as an act of war and one bomb in New York as an act of terrorism?

According to the *Oxford English Dictionary*, terrorism is 'a policy intended to strike with terror those against whom it is adopted' and a terrorist is 'any one who attempts to further his views by a system of coercive intimidation.' These definitions would apply to many tactical and strategic aspects of warfare and to many military and national leaders in wartime. The German air raids on Britain in the Second World War are one example of war by terror; the allied bombing of Germany, especially British night time bombing, is another. There are countless others: the nuclear destruction of the Japanese cities of Hiroshima and Nagasaki in August 1945 to end the Second World War; the Russian army's assault on Grozny, Chechnya, in January and February 1995; the ethnic cleansing of Bosnia-Herzegovina and Croatia in the wars of Yugoslavia's disintegration in the 1990s; and so on in grim succession.

Not all warfare is conducted with such ethical disregard. But the distinction between the violence that most people call war and the violence that most call terrorism is, it seems clear, not a fundamentally ethical distinction. The essential difference between war and terrorism is between violence unleashed by a state and violence unleashed by those outside and against the state. Terrorists usually have access to far smaller amounts of destructive power than do states.

This is another area in which the basic data are uncertain. The information bank maintained at St Andrew's University, Scotland, by Professor Paul Wilkinson is my source for the breakdown of terrorist incidents by type. This source records a considerably higher total of incidents and more fatalities than does the US State Department. Unlike St Andrew's, however, the latter's annual compilations do break down the incidents by country, which is why they are the source for the national totals in this map. Definitions of what constitutes an incident also vary, as to the way in which an incident is identified as domestic terrorism or international. In principle, whether an incident is classified as international should depend on whether the group that perpetrates it is acting within the territory of the state against which it is fighting. For example, an IRA bomb in London is domestic; an IRA bomb in Germany is international. Some close observers of this kind of violence suspect that the US State Department has the habit of defining an incident as international if – and sometimes only if – US citizens were among its actual or intended victims.

## 6 DEATH TOLL

Data on war deaths are supremely unreliable. Among the reasons for this are the propaganda needs of the contending sides. In most wars, there is no agency whose task it is to count the civilian dead who constitute the vast majority of war fatalities.

Estimates of casualties in Bosnia-Herzegovina illustrate the pitfalls. The most commonly used figure for war deaths in Bosnia in the war of 1992-95 is 200,000. In December 1992, Harris Silajdzic, who was at that time Bosnian Foreign Minister, claimed that 128,444 people had died on the Bosnian side alone. A couple of months earlier, a senior UN official had predicted that there would be 400,000 deaths. The figure of 200,000 emerged from the Bosnian Information Ministry in June 1993. For the next two and a half years of warfare, of fluctuating intensity, the same figure was used by almost all reporters, policy analysts and politicians. Occasionally, somebody would increase the estimate to 250,000, but there were never any takers: 200,000 was the safe figure, the common currency. Taken literally, this estimate means that in the first 14 months of war in Bosnia, some 470 people died each day on average; thereafter for a further 28 months, none. Taken literally, it means that the Muslim-Croat war never happened, nor the Serb offensives against Gorazde and Bihac, nor the 1995 atrocities in Zepa and Srebrenica.

Of course, the figure should not be taken literally. Such an estimate is not factual but human and political. The issue is not about statistics. Putting a figure to the number of deaths in Bosnia-Herzegovina was simply a shorthand from which the horror of what was happening could be easily understood.

How then is it possible to calculate a total number of war deaths worldwide and report it with any confidence? Only by comparing the information provided by different sources and treating the figures sceptically. The total reported in this atlas – five and a half million in the first half of the 1990s – is compiled from a variety of sources: the news media including international press agency reports, official sources, annual reference works, and the books and reports of other researchers including those who annually monitor the world's war situation, and those who focus on individual countries or regions. I have not used figures that seem clearly designed for propaganda, and I have rejected the highest estimates, though in only a few cases have I used the lowest one.

## 7 FEAR AND FLIGHT

A refugee has hitherto meant somebody who has fled his or her home with a well grounded fear for their safety and has crossed international borders. In recent years, an increasing number of people have been driven from their homes but have remained within their own country. In specialist circles, they are known as internally displaced people. Common usage has applied the term refugee to them. It is indeed only logical to acknowledge them as refugees and equally to acknowledge that there is an ethical responsibility to assist them just as much as international refugees. They are different only in where they went, not why they fled.

This map uses data from the most reliable of sources of information on refugees, the US Committee for Refugees. Information up to and including 1994 comes from its indispensable annual work of reference and analysis, World Refugee Survey. I am particularly grateful to the US Committee on Refugees for providing the figures for 1995 before they were finalized and published. The data problems here are similar to those encountered in estimating numbers of war casualties. On the one hand, there are usually objective and insurmountable problems in attempting to assess the numbers of internally displaced people, who are not crossing an international border. They may be displaced to areas that are still close to a war zone. The government or the insurgent leaders may not want to allow international observers access. Either side may want either to inflate the figures or reduce them for propaganda purposes.

Statistics on international refugees are often subject to a more or less straightforward negotiation between the host government and the UN High Commission for Refugees, since the host government in a poor country can expect to receive payment for each refugee. Even without making the most cynical assumptions about the process, it is immediately evident that one side has every interest in negotiating the figures up and the other has every reason to talk them down. It is the task of researchers at the US Committee for Refugees to pick their way through a thicket of such problems. One of the many strengths of the World Refugee Survey is that as well as international refugees and internally displaced people, it also includes those who live in refugee like circumstances. They are people who are refugees in every way except that they are not officially recognized as such. They have been included in the figures on which the cartogram is based.

## 8 LETHAL LEGACY

Landmines became the focus of international concern and campaigning in the mid 1990s, after decades during which they had caused tens of thousands of injuries and deaths. Landmines are cheap to buy and safe to sow in the ground; they are both expensive and dangerous to remove. Two aspects of landmine use are particularly ruthless. Firstly, many of the mines are too small to damage vehicles; they are intended only to kill or injure personnel. Indeed, one reason why some are particularly small is so that they will injure rather than kill, but injure seriously enough to overburden the adversary's military medical service. Secondly, mines – including anti personnel mines – are routinely sown not just to defend military installations, guerrilla camps and so on, but to terrorize the civilian population and prevent them working the fields and growing food. By intimidation and by removing the economic basis of rural communities' wellbeing, landmines can clear an area of non combatants, thus removing potential sources of information and support for the enemy.

Major international agencies including the United Nations and the International Red Cross and Red Crescent are now monitoring the landmine problem. As the information becomes clearer, the need for an international treaty that properly restricts the production and use of landmines becomes more striking.

## 9 THE DISINTEGRATION

The wars of Yugoslavia's disintegration from 1991 to 1995 were the largest armed conflict in Europe since the end of the Second World War. Alongside the violence and the human tragedies, the element of the wars that caused most comment was the faint response of outside powers. A great deal of moral rhetoric was expended about the wars and the war crimes in Croatia and Bosnia but, until 1995, little more.

There are three ways to interpret the four years of half hearted and inadequate international response to the wars of Yugoslavia, and especially the three years of ineffectiveness over Bosnia. The first explanation sees incompetence and indecision, based on a lack of proper information and analysis about what was happening and why. There is much evidence to support this view. It is hard to think of one stated, major goal of the Western powers that has been fulfilled. Among the abiding riddles of outside intervention is why the USA and its major allies have supported a resolution of the war based on ethnic cleansing and new boundaries that were established by force, when they began with the avowed aims of ensuring respect for legal borders and of punishing and reversing ethnic cleansing.

A second explanation is more charitable to the Western powers. It stresses the complexities of a major intervention in the war in Bosnia-Herzegovina. The terrain is difficult from a military point of view and the politics are intricate. Political objectives were hard either to identify or achieve and there was never any sign of willingness among Western public opinion to pay a high human or economic price. There were some who called for a quick fix, a US bombing raid or two. But bombing raids are less accurate than most people realize and some targets are particularly difficult to find and destroy. Moreover, as was shown when NATO air strikes in spring 1995 led to UN forces being taken hostage by Bosnian Serb forces, the decisive use of air power would only have been possible so long as UN forces were withdrawn from danger zones.

A third explanation of Western policy turns the argument on its head. In this interpretation, there was an active policy, implemented consistently, and largely successful. The aims of this policy were that the wars should not spill over into the rest of the Balkans; that the costs for the rest of Europe should be limited and few Western military personnel should lose their lives; and that after the war there should be a regional balance of power between Croatia and Serbia. In other words, *realpolitik* ruled. This interpretation focuses on the policies of the British and French governments from late 1991 until spring 1995.

In this view , the US administration was prepared to stay out of a complex and dangerous situation, until it came to seem that a foreign policy triumph could help President Clinton's re-election.

The Dayton agreement which the USA engineered is fragile and brings no certainty of either peace or justice. The cynics may or may not be right in their reading of British, French and US motives. They may turn out to be all too accurate in their reading of the problems of intervening effectively in the affairs of former Yugoslavia.

## 10 ETHNIC CLEANSING

The victors in former Yugoslavia are the extreme nationalists who believe, against all the evidence of the history of their own and every other nation, that it is impossible or undesirable (or both) for people from different ethnic groups to live together. They have achieved ethnic separation in small part because when war sweeps into a region, many people flee to the nearest relatively safe place they can find. But mostly they have achieved it as a result of deliberate policy. Those who pushed the policy of ethnic cleansing with greatest vigour and consistency were the Bosnian Serbs and their other Serbian allies. Those who suffered from it most were the Bosnian Muslims and those citizens of Bosnia-Herzegovina who could not or did not want to define themselves by any of these narrow ethnic labels. But all the main protagonists in the wars of Bosnia-Herzegovina and Croatia – Croat and Muslim forces as well as Serb – have perpetrated ethnic cleansing and committed atrocities.

Perhaps the most extraordinary episode of ethnic cleansing was in 1996 when the Bosnian Serb government cleared Sarajevo of Serbs, after the Dayton agreement, so that they would not live under a Muslim city administration. Serb politicians who once appeared on television to deny their forces were involved in ethnic cleansing against Muslims, now stepped forward to remark that Serbs were leaving Sarajevo because they felt unsafe. Meanwhile, teams of armed Serbian thugs roamed through the Serb areas of the city. They forced residents out, kicking them if they were too slow, burning the buildings so there would be nothing to come back to. The means were different, for this time there were no massacres, mass rapes or concentration camps to spread terror and accelerate the process, but the principle was the same. This was ethnic cleansing, directed by the Bosnian Serb government against its own. So too was the sudden exodus of Serbs from Krajina and Western Slavonia after the swift Croatian victories there in 1995. It was the ultimate logic of ethnic cleansing.

How can one understand this insistence on homogeneity at any price? Political analysts seek explanations in underlying interests and rational motives. Ethnic cleansing has a certain logic in maintaining the power of a narrow group, but there is something here that goes beyond rational politics and into psychotic fear. The economic reconstruction of the war torn parts of former Yugoslavia will be a difficult and expensive task. Attempting to build viable, lasting political structures will also be difficult. Hardest of all may be a cultural and psychological reconstruction to prevent future cycles of violence.

## 11 EDGE OF EMPIRE

Mikhail Gorbachev came to power in the USSR in 1985, with a reform programme that aimed to inject efficiency into a stagnant and ossified system. The most powerful political force unleashed by the attempted reforms was nationalism. The Soviet constitution defined the USSR as a Union (or federation) of 15 republics. Movements for independence grew in several of them. By 1991, five (Estonia, Latvia, Lithuania, Georgia and Tajikistan) had declared independence in principle and a civil war had begun over the status of Nagorno-Karabakh, the largely Armenian enclave within Azerbaijan. The attempted coup against Gorbachev in August 1991 was specifically intended to prevent the impending break up of the USSR, to deny the constituent republics the possibility to secede. Its failure merely hastened that very break up.

In the Caucasus, and elsewhere, the demise of the USSR paved the way to new problems in inter-group relations. The borders between the republics were designed to keep the national groups in the region in constant competition with each other, so that Moscow would remain the sole arbiter of their differences and disputes. In addition, partly because of large population movements (some forced), there was no clear match of national groups and national republics. Independence left plenty of aspirations unsatisfied and removed from the scene the only authority that was used to judging, however unsatisfactorily, the claims and interests of competing groups. The independence of Armenia and Azerbaijan simply intensified their war over Nagorno-Karabakh. The extreme nationalism of Zviad Ghamsakhurdia, who led Georgia to independence, quickly provoked demands for secession by Abkhazia and South Ossetia. The Chechen-Ingush Republic broke up into its two constituent parts. While Chechnya declared independence under the leadership of Dzhokhar Dudaev, the Ingush leaders preferred to remain in Russia in the hope that their new republic would be able to gain territory just north of Vladikavkaz. The area, Prigorodny raion, had once been Ingush but was placed under the jurisdiction of neighbouring North Ossetia at the time of the mass deportation in 1944. Though the Republic of Ingushetia was officially formed as part of the Russian Federation in 1992, its borders were not fixed. They remained uncertain in mid 1996, as this atlas went to press.

These are the conflicts that have turned violent. Yet there are other disputes and demands for recognition by ethno-national groups. There are several territorial disputes in the northern Caucasus within Russia that are also the consequence of the deportations of 1944 and the continued failure to resolve problems. The richest ethnic and national mix is in Dagestan: in the terminology of Russian ethnography, it contains 14 nationalities and 32 ethnic groups, in a total population of just two million. Many of these groups have demands and grievances. One group, the Lezgins, straddles the border with Azerbaijan. But in Dagestan there has been a more imaginative and subtle approach to the problem than in some other areas. No state language has been established, thus avoiding what is always a particularly sensitive issue. Instead, efforts are made to meet everybody's language needs with multi lingual newspapers, radio and television. Likewise, no state presidency has been created; instead, there is a parliamentary leadership in which every effort is made to maintain an ethnic balance.

Much of the research for this map was by Pavel Baev.

## 12 FROM WAR TO WAR

When the USSR invaded Afghanistan in December 1979, the Soviet leadership thought it was sending in troops for a quick fix to deal with a spot of local trouble. In the event, the invasion hastened the end of a relatively calm period in US-Soviet relations. Detente ended and a new phase of the Cold War began. And the long commitment of forces into what the Soviet leadership took many years to admit was a full scale war, helped weaken its legitimacy at home, its authority and its will to rule. For all this, the withdrawal of Soviet forces in 1989 did not bring an end to the Afghan war.

The war in Afghanistan is a classic case of a war whose causes change over time. What began as a struggle to resist modernization by an essentially feudal segment of society became, after the Soviet invasion, a war of independence which, in turn, became a war to overthrow the pro-Moscow government and, finally, a war between the victors. Since ethnic Tajik forces took Kabul in April 1992, it has been the main target of the fighting between shifting coalitions of warlords.

To the north, Tajikistan has become caught in a similar situation. With no group powerful enough to win a decisive victory, and with no coalition yet having emerged that is capable of achieving political stability, if they are even interested in it, warfare ceases to have any objective. The point of war has become war itself.

Much of the research for this map was by Pavel Baev.

## 13 NATIONLESS NATION

The Gulf War of 1991 between Iraq and the international coalition led by the USA, was followed by two uprisings within Iraq, in the south by the Shi'a minority and in the north by Iraqi Kurds. Both uprisings were eventually defeated by Saddam Hussein's forces while the Western powers, which had seemed to promise to support the overthrow of the Iraqi dictator, stood by. The West, having ejected Iraqi forces from Kuwait, wanted Iraq to remain intact. Western leaders would have been happy for Saddam Hussein to be overthrown, but not if it meant dismembering Iraq. So once again, Kurdish dreams of an independent Kurdistan were sacrificed for the grand strategy of outside powers. As hundreds of thousands of refugees fled the advancing Iraqi forces, the West did at least manage to mount a major humanitarian operation. In the north of Iraq, safe havens were established and a 'no fly zone' was imposed — a line north of which Iraqi military flights were banned.

It is ironic that Turkey thus became a key player in a humanitarian operation for Kurds. At its foundation, modern Turkey's nationalist ideology allowed room for only one identity, and those who resisted it have been persecuted. They have been culturally excluded, denied political freedoms, forced from their homes or even massacred. In Turkey, Kurds were for a long time forbidden to refer to themselves as Kurds, the officially acceptable term being 'mountain Turk'. Unlike Iraqi governments, including Saddam Hussein's, which have always recognized and often celebrated Kurdish identity, Turkish governments made every effort to wipe out Kurdishness, banning Kurdish holidays, festivals and distinctively Kurdish styles of dress, and refusing to allow the Kurdish language to be taught in schools. The emphasis placed on using schooling as a means of assimilating Kurds explains why the armed Kurdistan Workers' Party (PKK) carries out terror attacks against schools and teachers.

The map showing the proposed extent of Kurdistan in the Treaty of Sèvres refers to 'Ottoman Turkey'. That was not a technically correct name but a reasonable compromise. The Ottoman empire was effectively ended, having lost almost all territories outside Anatolia as a result of defeat in the First World War. The Republic of Turkey was formed in 1923, three years after the Treaty of Sèvres had been signed.

## 14 HOLY LANDS

Secret negotiations in 1993 paved the way to an historic agreement between the Israeli government and the Palestine Liberation Organization in September that year. Though it put some parts of the Palestinian territory under Palestinian control, it was not an all encompassing peace agreement but it was a framework for progress and accord. In 1995 there was a further agreement, placing more areas under Palestinian control. In early 1996, there was an initial agreement on sharing water rights. All the same, armed conflict continued.

Since the 1993 agreement, the overriding question has always been whether such an opportunity for peace would be seized. Immediately after Yitzhak Rabin was assassinated in 1995, it did seem as if Israeli voters would choose to continue the quest for peace. Indeed, Rabin was remembered as a peace idealist, rather than the hard headed realist he was. Rabin believed that negotiation and compromise were better roads to security than a state run on military police lines. His main weakness in relation to the peace process was his tendency to treat the 1993 agreement as a Palestinian surrender. The 1996 election brought the conservative Binyamin Netanyahu to power. Perhaps there had been too much idealization of Rabin, or perhaps there had been too little trust in his successor, Shimon Peres, or maybe Netanyahu's success was simply the result of a new escalation of conflict in Israel and in southern Lebanon. But it remained an open question whether the opportunity for peace would be taken.

Netanyahu may take a harder line on some negotiating questions than his immediate predecessors, but he is no more able than they to use military means to destroy and disarm the Palestinian opposition. It is not a question of will but of feasibility. On the other side, the Islamists of Hezbollah, Hamas and Islamic Jihad will not succeed in breaking the Israeli state by using armed strength any more than could the PLO – or, indeed, any more than could Arab governments in four wars from Israel's foundation until 1973.

In 1993, both sides understood that neither could win. Yet recognizing that simple truth has complex implications and the choice of peace is often more difficult for those most closely involved than it seems to outside observers. By mid 1996, when this atlas went to press, the choice for or against peace had not been made.

## 15 MILITANT FAITH

The defining feature of political Islam (or Islamism) is the contention that Islam possesses a theory of politics and the state and of how they should be organized. The varied Islamist movements and organizations became the most dynamic political force in the Middle East during the 1980s. Their influence is felt from Europe to the Philippines and in sub Saharan Africa. In many Islamic countries, the state claims to rule according to Islam and in many the judicial system is based on Islamic legal principles. But Islamist regimes are those that base their constitution on the Koran.

Political Islam is but one of several possible modes within Islam. Its current strength comes from economic, political and cultural sources. In the Arab world, the economic problem begins with how wealth is used. Wealth in some parts is spectacular but it is not spread very widely. In Kuwait and Saudi Arabia, national income per head of population is at West European levels but the overall level of development is more like Latin America's. In both richer and poorer Arab countries, the basic problems derive from the way in which their national economies are integrated into the world economy. The Arab role in the world economy is limited to oil and, more recently, the deployment of financial capital. No Arab country is a major exporter of manufactured commodities. With the exception of a narrow elite, the Arab world is as economically powerless now as it was a hundred years ago. This exacerbates the deeply problematic relationship between rulers and ruled. The lack of genuine democracy is symptomatic of the lack of legitimacy of governments whose rule is based on the systematic exclusion and marginalization of the majority.

Political opposition has been channelled primarily through the Islamist movements in recent years for three reasons. Firstly, faith and politics have a tendency to walk hand in hand. In the context of a political community of the faithful, it is almost a matter of cultural instinct to see political and religious renewal as two parts of a single process. Secondly, religion provides political shelter. Mosques are often the only places where independent political organization and mobilization are possible. Thirdly, for those who seek a focus for opposition, there is no real alternative. Of the other political voices that oppose current regimes, none has the ringing certainty, the cohesion and the mass appeal of the Islamists.

This map, like **17 Land Lords**, shows incidents of mass, violent protest against economic austerity programmes. These are economic packages that include cuts in government spending, which lead to rising food and transport prices as subsidies are cut, and to the laying off of large numbers of state employees. In most cases, it is the price increases that trigger violent protest. Most of the austerity programmes are inspired by the International Monetary Fund or the World Bank and are often linked to agreements on debt repayment.

## 16 AFTER THE RAJ

Mahatma Gandhi was the foremost leader and living symbol of the struggle against British rule in the Indian sub continent. During the 1920s and 1930s, he led the region to independence, pioneering non violent political tactics. Gandhi's name is synonymous with peace. Yet one paradox of modern history is that this peaceful path to independence turned into a bloodbath at the very moment of its success.

Since independence both domestic and international politics within the region have been scarred by persistent violence and warfare. Behind the internal conflicts there lies a combination of economic inequality and ethnic division. In India, Pakistan and Sri Lanka, as elsewhere, it often proves easier for politicians to mobilize support by taking a strong line in favour of their own ethnic group. In Sri Lanka at the time of independence, the Tamil minority held a disproportionate number of official positions in the government administration. By itself, this need not have led to the violence of the civil war since the late 1970s. But Sinhalese politicians vied with each other in anti Tamil rhetoric and policies and unknowingly set the country on its path to ethnic civil war. In India, even after the violence of partition, when many Muslims left India and many Hindus arrived from Pakistan, communal violence was neither inevitable nor immediate. In the 1990s, religion has become a major organizing principle in politics and, for some, any means are acceptable to advance their politico-religious cause. In Pakistan, religious division within Islam, between Sunni and Shi'a devotees, has similarly emerged as a means of political organization, closely connected to the eruption of violence and terror.

Burma is different. Through half a century of independence, there have been four or five separatist armed conflicts in any one year. The military dictatorship in Rangoon lacks all legitimacy and exists only to maintain the privilege of a small elite. To that end, it uses war, torture and assassination. For building a railway, it uses slavery. Yet all through the former Raj there are leaders who speak from a democratic tradition for tolerance, pluralism and respect for human rights and dignity. Outstanding but not alone is Aung San Suu Kyi, who emerged in 1988 as the leader of Burma's democratic movement.

## 17 LAND LORDS

If democracy is to work over a long period, more is needed than formal rights and a trip to the polls every few years. A democratic political culture is also essential. This means people understanding and accepting the rules of the game, agreeing to disagree, in the knowledge that the party that wins a few more votes will not be brutal in its success and with the security that the losing parties will accept the verdict and not challenge it by violence. Such tolerant acceptance of pluralism in society and politics is never easy to nurture. It seems to be least difficult when people are prosperous and economically secure, especially if the prosperity is shared among a relatively large proportion of the population.

There are some parts of the world where it seems as though a democratic political culture could never take root. There are areas, as in most of Latin America, where it has taken root among some groups but not among others. The culture of democracy is strong among much of the middle class and the urban working class. However, the prosperous elite in rural areas, the large landowners and the armed forces have permitted only a show of democracy – which lasts only so long as the outcome does not contradict their interests or threaten their privilege. When several of the dictatorships in Latin America were removed in the 1980s – in Argentina, Brazil and Chile among others – the issue of democracy was left finely poised. Those dictatorships had been unusually brutal, and particularly efficient at dismantling and destroying many of the elements of civil society on which a democratic culture must be based. Formal democracy was restored but the competition between opposing viewpoints and interests was still tilted in one side's favour. The organizational structure for those who would stand up and oppose injustices in the existing order had been weakened, while a willingness to stand up was constrained by the knowledge of what happened under the old dictatorships. Such memories are made more pertinent by the amnesties offered to officers who played key roles for the dictatorships; the former dictators and their subordinates are still lurking in the wings. In many rural areas of Latin America, the law of the strongest and most violent is the only law that counts.

This map shows incidents of mass, violent protest against economic austerity programmes. The note to **15 Militant Faith**, gives some background about these programmes and protests.

Much of the research for this map was by Wenche Hauge.

## 18 THE DISPOSSESSION

The European powers who snatched 85 percent of Africa during the course of 20 years abandoned 80 percent of it in the 25 years from 1955 to 1980.

Most African countries have been independent since the 1960s, but they have been largely unable to surmount their colonial history. This was a brutal experience, an extended process of dispossession, an attack on social organization and cultural norms, characterized not only by conquest but in many places by determined and extended resistance. The colonial authorities systematically denied human dignity and rights, including the right to life itself. Such a massive trauma cannot be thrown off in just a generation or two. Few African countries have been able to give their citizens economic, political and human security since they gained independence. Meanwhile, the major powers have continued to use Africa as a source of natural resources and primary commodities, although in many cases the resources now of greatest interest have changed from colonial times. They continue to treat African countries as colonies, but have shed the burden of running them.

In the West, the attitudes of the key commodity brokers and financial investors are clear: they see no reason to import anything from Africa except for primary commodities and no reason to invest except to extract raw materials. Africans are not expected to manufacture goods for the world market. When national economies depend on exporting raw materials, fluctuating prices of primary commodities can have a major effect on long term economic prospects. Nigeria's political trajectory towards military dictatorship was decisively affected by the collapse in oil prices in the 1980s. Zambia, whose economy had already been hurt by the need to impose sanctions on Rhodesia from 1966, suffered later from a collapse in copper prices. Burundi and Rwanda were both hit hard by the collapse in coffee prices at the end of the 1980s. The 1980s were a catastrophic period for the whole continent. Africa's share of the world export market fell from 2.4 percent to 1.4 percent. Its share of world exports of non oil primary commodities fell from 7 percent to 4 percent and foreign investment declined in proportion. Total external debt rose from less than 30 percent of Africa's combined Gross National Product to more than 100 percent. The average share of export earnings spent on paying the interest on external debt rose from 13 percent to over 30 percent. This meant that the net flow of financial resources was not into the world's poorest continent but out of it. As a result, Africa's conflicts continued and worsened in the 1990s.

It is probably unrealistic for Africa to expect real assistance from a world which has dealt it so much damage. But conditions for social and economic development would be much improved if the rich of the world were to desist from continuing to take Africa's economic resources.

## 19 THE DISPOSSESSED

The lingering impact of colonialism (see note to **18 The Dispossession**) does not justify the acts of inhumanity that have been witnessed in some parts of the continent in recent years. While Burundi and Rwanda (see **20 Times for Killing**) are two countries that may immediately spring to mind, West Africa displays a similar combination of poverty, dictatorship and conflict on a geographically larger scale. Through the 1980s, several countries experienced growth in debt, decline in wealth and the stifling of democracy. In their wake came war. But beginning in 1990, a wave of struggles for democracy swept through Burkina Faso, Cameroon, Côte d'Ivoire, Gabon and Nigeria. In Nigeria, democracy was suppressed. Elsewhere there were some victories for those demanding democracy, though in some cases the results have been more cosmetic than substantial – the leaders changed but the problems persisted. They will continue to persist, unless there is movement on basic economic questions as well as the political front.

In order to calculate the number of years spent under military dominated governments, I have not confined myself to years in which governments were headed by serving or recently retired senior military officers. Among military dominated governments, there are some that are headed by civilians who are dependent on active support from the military establishment for their survival. This is, therefore, a more inclusive definition than, for example, 'military dictatorship' or 'military regime', and thus catches some cases in which the real power hides behind a convenient front.

## 20 TIMES FOR KILLING

The 1994 massacres in Rwanda set standards of horror unparalleled since the Cambodia massacres in the mid 1970s. For the mass media and for an aghast world public, the massacres broke without warning. Yet the war had already been going on for three and a half years, and early in 1994 Rwandan army officers were boasting about their ability to kill at the rate of a thousand people every 20 minutes. Although in the end many and perhaps the majority of killings were with machetes and knives, and seemingly carried out at random, the massacres began with systematic killing by well armed soldiers carrying lists of those to be executed. It has since been confirmed that warning signs of the coming disaster were either ignored or misinterpreted.

Observers and experts have warned that Burundi will be next but in one way, the warning is already too late. The massacres in Burundi in October 1993 were followed by month after month of further killings, at a lesser rate, but adding up to the murder of tens of thousands of people. Against a background of economic instability, land shortages and a lack of stable democracy, Burundi and Rwanda have become caught up in a repetitive cycle of violence. The massacres since independence have left fear and hatred behind them and an expectation that political differences can only be settled by violence. In such circumstances it takes vision and bravery to seek reconciliation. Boutros Boutros Ghali, the UN Secretary-General, identified the problem precisely when he told a group of Burundian politicians, 'Your enemy is not each other but fear and cowardice. You must have the courage to accept compromise.'

The enormous mineral resources of Zaire have brought wealth only to its dictator, President Mobutu, and those closest to him. Even the army has rioted because of lack of pay in recent years. With such potential natural wealth, it has taken corruption and mismanagement on an epic scale to make Zaire one of the world's thirty poorest countries. The regime maintains its power through repression and an all pervasive climate of fear. Even so, in the first half of the 1990s, it was only the regime's willingness to stir up ethnic clashes that prevented the majority from taking the terrible risk of an uprising against the state. The same tactic was used in Kenya in the early 1990s to stave off the challenge of democracy.

## 21 HORN OF POVERTY

The surprising message from the Horn of Africa is that progress is possible against all odds. Surprising because, in the 1980s, thanks to the international public alert sounded by reports on the famine in Ethiopia and the response of 'Band Aid' and other major acts of charity, the Horn became the symbol of everything that was wrong and hopeless in Africa. A decade later, the situation is hardly better in Somalia and Sudan. It is considerably improved but still fragile in Uganda, where the religious anti-government forces in the north changed their name between 1992 and 1993 from the Holy Spirit Movement to the Lord's Resistance Army. And in Djibouti and Kenya the situation has temporarily stabilized after a serious deterioration.

In Eritrea and Ethiopia, despite many complications, the always provisional balance sheet looked rather more positive. In both countries, the governments attempted to take the opportunity offered by the end of the long wars to address some of the basic economic and environmental problems. When Eritrea clashed with Yemen about territorial jurisdiction over islands in the Red Sea, equally when the Ethiopian government was unable to find a peaceful solution to conflicts in the Ogaden region, or to settle disputes with Oromo leaders and attract them into the enterprise of reconstructing the country, it was immediately evident how daunting and complex the task will be. But at least a start has been made. When berating a group of Burundian politicians (see note to **20 Times for Killing**), UN Secretary-General Boutros Boutros Ghali concluded his homily with the words, 'You must assume your responsibilities. If you don't, nobody will save you.' If there are grounds for hope in some parts of the Horn of Africa, it is because some political leaders have at last begun to assume their responsibilities.

## 22 ISLANDS OF CONFLICT

East Asia was a central battleground in the Cold War from 1945 until the mid 1980s. Today, the old ideological dividing lines have almost completely lost their meaning. Vietnam exemplifies this change.

The USA's war in Vietnam ended in a humiliation of frustrated power and national division that cast a long shadow after the US military withdrawal in 1973 and the defeat, in 1975, of regimes installed by the USA in South Vietnam and Cambodia. But in the mid 1990s, less than twenty years later, investment capital has moved in along with credit cards and fast food. Like other governments in the region, the Vietnamese government decided that its country's future lay in a low wage economy with a disciplined labour force doing the work that transnational corporations now find it too costly in economic, ecological or human terms to have done in richer countries. South Korea, Singapore, Taiwan and Hong Kong have all provided the West with a pool of cheap labour. As a result, these countries have been able to develop large corporations and booming economies – as well as some savage ecological problems. The Philippines, Indonesia, Malaysia and Thailand all followed suit with varying degrees of success. So too, in restricted areas, have China and Vietnam.

The dwindling importance of Cold War ideology became evident even earlier. In 1974, the year before the Communist victory in Vietnam, China sent forces to occupy some of the Paracel Islands. In 1979, Communist China sent forces across the border into Communist Vietnam, which itself had dislodged the Communist regime in Cambodia. In 1996, Vietnam has more in common with Indonesia, Malaysia, the Philippines and Taiwan, all of whom want to prevent China from taking sole control of the Spratly archipelago.

Two armed conflicts still reflect the old dividing lines – in the Philippines between the government and the Communist New People's Army, and in Cambodia where the Khmer Rouge remain active (see **29 In the Shadow of Massacre**). Even the tensions between China and Taiwan (where the defeated anti-Communist nationalists took power in 1949) cannot be interpreted through the old ideological lens. Today, the issues are about regional power and the control of territory. The Chinese government wants Taiwan back as part of China for the same reason that it wants Hong Kong and Macau; it sees these territories as inextricably Chinese.

This map combines the many wars in Burma. For more details see **16 After the Raj**.

## 23 UNDER ARMS

The number of men and women under arms fell by 15 percent from the mid 1980s to the mid 1990s. This fall illustrates two aspects of change in military forces in the 1990s. Following the end of the Cold War, the armed forces of several states were reduced quite sharply. The second cause of change is not related to disarmament. Among the richest states, military power has become increasingly technology intensive over the half century since the Second World War. It is not only the number of military personnel, but the technological capability of their equipment and the skill and precision with which they can use it, that determines military capacity. Three key advances in the 1980s were the introduction of extremely fast computers, decisive improvements in targeting techniques, and big steps forward in the ability to monitor events on the battlefield. These technologies combined to give the states with access to them – primarily the USA and its closest allies – military preponderance over key opponents, regardless of who had the numerical advantage. As technology becomes more sophisticated, so it becomes more expensive. Thus, relentless technological advance both enables and puts pressure on states to reduce their military personnel; they can neither afford nor do they need such numbers of people as before.

It seems likely that technological developments will encourage the slow trend away from mass conscript armies. Some conscript forces no longer need to draft every able bodied male of the appropriate age. Some countries, most notably Russia, try to draft them all but fail. France, correctly shown on the map as a conscript country, has announced a switch to all volunteer forces. Others will almost certainly follow. One likely result is an increase in the proportion of women in the military. In six states, women make up more than five percent of the total military personnel. The forces of five of those six are volunteer. The exception is Russia. Women used to make up a mere 0.02 percent of Soviet military personnel until young men started to refuse to respond to the annual draft, at first because of the war in Afghanistan, later because the USSR was beginning to fall apart. Well documented stories of systematic abuse and mistreatment of new recruits continue to fuel a high rate of rejection of the annual Russian draft, strengthened by the fear and opposition roused by the Russian war in Chechnya.

Armed forces are slowly and only partially overcoming their reluctance to employ women. And when they do, they deploy women in medicine, communications and administration rather than in combat roles.

There are only rough estimates of the size of insurgent armed forces. The available information indicates that they constitute just under five percent of the world total of all armed forces. Among other imprecisions in the data, the estimated number of young soldiers is especially unreliable.

The length of service in conscript forces often varies between the different services. Sometimes it varies between ethnic groups. There is no consistent principle on which this is organized: in some countries it seems that the unfavoured ethnic group is punished with long service; in others such a group is apparently regarded as unreliable and so has a shorter term to serve. The length of service may also be altered as a result of war – and sometimes it varies at random. In all such cases, the period shown by the colour on the map is the longest period, because that is the burden of duty that a young male risks carrying as he grows up.

The source for this map is *The Military Balance*, the annual compilation of the London-based International Institute for Strategic Studies. For some states it does not indicate how long conscripts serve; I have arbitrarily assigned those states the colour that indicates a term of less than one year.

## 24 MILITARY SPENDING

As military spending fell in the early 1990s, 'the peace dividend' was the name given to the opportunity to redirect resources released from the military sector. These resources could be used for prosperity and profit, for aid to poorer countries or for environmental protection. In the first flush of the end of the Cold War, hopes and expectations were rather too large. Disarmament itself costs money, both to monitor compliance with agreements, and to render unwanted military equipment unusable. The promised peace dividend has thus turned out to be rather a disappointment. It is not clear how far cuts in military spending have improved the world economy, or even the economies of those countries which made the largest spending cuts. The estimated accumulated saving of one and a half trillion US dollars by the end of the century is a large amount of money in anybody's terms. But averaged over a decade, it is hardly more than half a percent of world economic output. Despite the intensive use of science and technology in the military sector, it is too much to expect that a peace dividend on that scale will have a widespread and decisive effect.

The peace dividend calculation I have used is modelled on the one in the UNDP's *Human Development Report 1994*. This calculation assumes that, were it not for the end of the Cold War, states would have continued to spend each year the same as they did in 1989 – the same, that is, in real terms, which means that the number of dollars might have risen but what they could buy would not change. In fact, military spending had already fallen from the peak it achieved in the first half of the 1980s. Whether it would have started to rise again, continued to fall or gone into a steady state cannot be known. The idea of the peace dividend is therefore a classic 'what if' concept – but worthwhile for all that as a way of understanding global political choices.

Comparing military spending across countries is a complex exercise. Even if one assumes that governments report their own spending accurately (despite the fact that some lie and some do not know), constructing a single measuring stick is virtually impossible. The free movements of goods, services and labour on the basis of which ordinary exchange rates are calculated do not apply in this sector. Inflation rates are different in the military and civilian sectors. The standard measure of value is the US dollar. Fluctuations in the exchange rate value of the dollar therefore have an important effect on calculations of total world spending and comparisons from one country to another. Thus, as with so much of the information in this atlas, what we are dealing with are educated estimates.

The source for the data on this cartogram is *The Military Balance*, produced annually by the International Institute for Strategic Studies in London. The *Yearbook* of the Stockholm International Peace Research Institute (SIPRI) used to be a better source but, in recent years, SIPRI has become somewhat too cautious for the purposes of an exercise such as this cartogram, leaving too many gaps in the information it presents, on the reasonable grounds that it does not wish to put forward data that are not just shaky but positively flaky. *The Military Balance* is bolder than the SIPRI *Yearbook* and offers fuller coverage.

Calculations of changes in military spending from 1985 to 1994 for states that emerged from former Czechoslovakia, former Yugoslavia and former USSR are based on a simple calculation of per capita military spending in 1985. For example, given the USSR's estimated military spending in 1985 (an uncertain, disputed and politically sensitive figure), what was Armenia's 'share', based on the percentage of the USSR's population that lived in Armenia? The answer provides the basis for comparison with Armenia's military spending in 1994. This lets us compare the choices about military spending made by independent Armenia with the choices made by the state from which it emerged. The result is a guide to the political choices of the new states and a way to compare the economic burden of military spending during and since the Cold War.

## 25 MARKET FORCES

The international trade in major weapons boomed in the late 1970s and the first half of the 1980s. Trade was fuelled in part by the surge in oil prices, in part by political and strategic rivalries, and in part by the needs of arms industries to keep finding new markets. In the second half of the 1980s the bubble burst and by the mid 1990s no recovery was in sight.

These figures cover the trade between governments in new major weapons such as tanks, aircraft and missiles. The figures do not include most of the trade involving sales to insurgent forces, which includes a significant trade in used weapon systems, and nor do they cover the trade in light weapons, about which there is a lack of systematic information. In some regions, the dissemination of light weapons is extraordinary. Among them is southern Africa, where the end of wars in Mozambique and the relative de-escalation of warfare in Angola are making rifles available for a few dollars. They are sold at a 4,000 percent profit in Johannesburg and other South African cities. There is a dark side to the outbreak of peace.

Afghanistan is also awash with light weapons. US supplies alone to the Mujahideen in the 1980s included over one million Kalashnikov rifles, according to some estimates. Together with rocket grenades, mortars light missiles and the like, these weapons came in through a supply channel that was leaky in the extreme. The recipients did not always use the weapons as intended. Many were stolen and sold to anybody who could afford the modest price — fighters in other wars, bandits, worried merchants and private citizens. Also for sale were weapons captured, stolen and bought from the Soviet army in Afghanistan from 1979 to 1989. Weapons imports continued into the 1990s as the war went on and the supply channels continue to leak.

The proliferation of light weapons is similarly intense throughout the southern belt of the former USSR, from the western shores of the Black Sea, through the Caucasus and into Central Asia. The arms market in Chechnya from 1991 to 1994 was the most notorious node in the dissemination of these weapons, but by no means the only one. Though light weapons have reportedly been imported into Chechnya via Turkey, the main source of supply was the Soviet army just before its break up and the Russian army since 1991. In July 1995, the Chechen forces of the late General Dzhokar Dudaev and the Russian government agreed to a ceasefire and to a disarmament process, in which it was agreed to pay the Chechens for every weapon they turned in. The disarmament process broke down within a few months because many of the Chechen fighters simply used the money to buy new weapons – usually two new guns for the price of the old one. Their suppliers were Russian soldiers standing only a few metres from the collection points.

The information available about the trade in light weapons is little more than anecdotal. An effort to establish a worldwide gun control system to police and restrict the trade will have to begin with a massive effort to identify and monitor it. The figures for major weapons are more accurate. The Stockholm International Peace Research Institute has been tracking the trade in major weapons for some 30 years. Its estimates take into account the usual problems of uncertain data and the difficulty of comparing military costs between countries. As a source, SIPRI's figures remain preferable to the UN arms trade register, which is based on voluntary reporting by governments and therefore contains many gaps.

## 26 THE ABC OF WEAPONS

During the Cold War, huge efforts were expended on stockpiling unusable weapons. In the early 1980s people in positions of power began to speak and act as if they did not respect that inhibition, and the sense of nuclear danger was at its most intense. A movement of international protest mobilized against the deployment of new generations of nuclear weapons. It failed to stop the new weapons but it changed the terms of debate. By 1987 and 1988, when Soviet leader Mikhail Gorbachev began his radical disarmament diplomacy, Western public opinion was ready for major cuts in nuclear weapons.

Despite being unusable, nuclear weapons had been deployed in almost every conceivable form. Among the components of the superpowers' nuclear arsenals were ground based, air launched, ship launched and submarine launched missiles; bombs on board aircraft; nuclear shells for army artillery; nuclear anti aircraft missiles; nuclear torpedoes; nuclear depth charges to attack undersea targets; atomic demolition munitions (ADMs) – remote controlled nuclear landmines; and the so-called backpack or suitcase ADM, so named because it was meant to be small enough to be carried by one man. Neither biological nor chemical gas weapons were integrated into military forces in the same way.

Against the disarmament trend, the proliferation of missiles continues. During the 1990s, a handful of new states is known to have brought conventional (that is, non-nuclear) missiles with ranges over 40 kilometres into their arsenals. Technologically advanced states worry that their military superiority will steadily be eroded. But it seems likely they can prevent the spread of missiles to new states only by curbing their own appetites.

The estimate of nuclear warhead numbers in this map represents a compromise between the most generally accepted estimates in the reference literature. I include the assessment, which is still controversial in some quarters, that Israel is a nuclear equipped state. India and Pakistan, however, seem more likely to have nuclear material that could be quickly assembled into deliverable weapons (missile warheads or bombs, for example), than to have nuclear bombs and missile warheads in their current, active inventory.

Whether these weapons can provide security and, if so, what kind of security, remains both controversial and unclear. South Africa's nuclear readiness could not protect the apartheid system, for example. And the abandonment of nuclear weapons potential by South Africa and by Brazil reflects a long term vision of security founded on democracy instead of military power.

## 27 DUMPING GROUNDS

In the first years of the atomic age, almost all nuclear testing was above ground. The few exceptions were nuclear test explosions under water. In 1955, the USA conducted the first underground nuclear test. In 1963, the Partial Test Ban Treaty was signed by the USA, the UK and the USSR. This banned nuclear test explosions in the atmosphere, under water, in space or in any environment if radioactive debris from the explosion crossed a national boundary. This did not stop the arms race but it helped clean up the atmosphere. It did not, however, come soon enough to save some Pacific atolls being rendered uninhabitable – Bikini is the best known – or to prevent long term genetic effects from the era of testing. France, which had begun nuclear testing in 1960, and China, which was to begin in 1965, did not sign the 1963 treaty. France, however, conducted its last above ground nuclear test in 1974; China's last test above ground was in 1980.

In the midst of the activity of military organizations, as in all human activity, accidents will happen. This is why almost 60 nuclear weapons and nuclear submarine reactors have been lost at sea. In few places have more such accidents happened, and nowhere is there a higher risk of further accidents, than northern Russia in the region of the Kola Peninsula, Murmansk, and the Barents Sea. In the first two or three years after the dissolution of the USSR, the Russian authorities appeared eager to cooperate with Western partners in identifying and charting the scale of the environmental disaster that had been perpetrated, and in estimating the extent of further risks. An agreement to work together for regional development between Finland, Norway, Russia and Sweden, gives a central role to environmental cooperation. However, in 1995 and 1996, Russian military and civilian government authorities appeared to start regarding the question as a matter of national sovereignty. The interest of outsiders in gaining key information on environmental risks started to be depicted as interference. Acknowledging the scale of the problem became an apparent surrender of national pride. But the principle at stake here is simple: averting the environmental disaster that stalks the northern seas is possible only if there is open information.

## 28 THE CALCULUS OF SECURITY

US-Soviet relations dominated world politics for nearly half a century after the end of the Second World War. The end of that long confrontation – which began with the dissolution of the USSR's alliance system in central and eastern Europe in 1989 and was completed with the dissolution of the USSR itself in 1991 – marked a watershed in world history. NATO had been the cornerstone of the Western security system and of US world power for over 40 years. The alliance's unity and sense of purpose were based on a set of four interlinked political and strategic assumptions. They were, firstly, that the USSR was a strategic threat to Western Europe and to other key regions such as northeast Asia; secondly, that resisting that threat depended on alliance unity; thirdly, that alliance unity was possible only under US leadership; and finally, that resisting the threat depended on both conventional and nuclear deterrence.

The end of the Cold War and the demise of the USSR were not only a triumph but also a challenge for this system of security and power. For, without the Soviet threat, what could hold the system together? In the early 1990s, NATO was faced with a choice that is unlikely to be resolved for a long time. On the one hand, it could try to be the old NATO without the old enemy – which implies an anxious search for a new enemy. Perhaps the new threat against which the alliance would bind together in the old way could be Saddam Hussein of Iraq? Perhaps, more generally, the Arab world or Islam? Or, if the reform process went wrong in Russia, perhaps a new enemy might emerge there? Especially if the Communists got a grip on power. Or the nationalists. NATO policy makers have often been eager pessimists.

NATO's other option was to find a genuinely new role. It could aim to prevent conflict at source rather than deter the use of force, and attempt to bring stability to Europe and its surrounding regions through cooperation. This role implies a search for new allies rather than new enemies, and for new opportunities to cooperate with a wider group of partners rather than a new threat. However, before NATO's new role was resolved, it was launched on the path of expansion. It now faces the prospect of growth, not simply of survival.

Much of the research for this map was by Pavel Baev.

## 29 IN THE SHADOW OF MASSACRE

The USA and North Vietnam between them precipitated the war in Cambodia that began in 1970. North Vietnam used routes through Cambodia to supply Communist forces in the South. US aircraft bombed the supply lines, but US commanders came to believe there was also a major Communist base somewhere in Cambodia.

The Cambodian leader, Prince Sihanouk, tried to hedge his bets, giving full support to neither the USA nor the North Vietnamese. In 1970, the US overthrew him and installed the pro American Lon Nol. His unpopularity only served to strengthen what had hitherto been a marginalized political force, the Khmer Rouge.

It is possible that the full human costs of the Khmer Rouge's victory in 1975 will never be known. Initial estimates were in the order of one million people killed – for political reasons, or as punishment and warnings to the rest of the population, or dying in famine provoked by the Khmer Rouge itself, which forcibly moved populations just at the moment when the 1975 harvest should have been gathered. In 1996, new estimates emerged, tripling the total to a scarcely credible three million, not far short of half the population. Despite its crimes, the Khmer Rouge was recognized by the USA and its allies as the legitimate government and representative of Cambodia, after it had been toppled by Vietnamese forces.

The UN has received such bad press for its role in Bosnia-Herzegovina and Somalia (see **32 Keeping Peace**) that it is worth remembering its role in Cambodia to stress the capacities of the organization. Certainly, the UN operation was not perfect, and many insiders and close observers complained about the quality of leadership within the UN itself. The impact of foreign troops and police officers arriving in Phnom Penh had some negative effects, not least on inflation and prostitution. But the operation ultimately met its objectives in extremely difficult circumstances and amid great danger. Having massacred between 15 and 50 percent of the population, the Khmer Rouge did not draw the line at kidnapping and assassinating UN soldiers and police in an effort to distort the election and rig the results. Fifty one states contributed to the UN operation in Cambodia. They did not have to contribute. And they might not have succeeded. But they did.

## 30 THE ORANGE AND THE GREEN

In August 1969, the annual Apprentice Boys march in Derry (Londonderry) precipitated violent riots in the Catholic area of Bogside. Among the rioters were the police, especially the B-Special reserves. The British government responded by bringing in the army to keep order. This was a popular move in mainland Britain. And in Derry, the troops were greeted with cups of tea and biscuits by relieved Bogside residents. Richard Crossman, a UK government minister at the time, wrote in his diary, 'We have now got into something we can hardly mismanage.'

It was almost thirty years before any British politician dared think with any optimism about Northern Ireland. If the peace process can succeed it will be because the centuries of conflict do not continue to retain their grip on people's loyalties and imaginations. There are so many resentments, so many wrongs and and so much revenge, that history – always selectively remembered by each side – simply gets in the way of a peaceful settlement.

## 31 LANDS OF GOOD HOPE

In the 1980s, South Africa was characterized at home by rigid apartheid and a conflict that was violent and escalating, and abroad by military intervention in the region and isolation on the international stage. Both the country and region have come a long way since then but the goodwill generated by peace and democratization in Southern Africa does not guarantee success.

In August 1990 the African National Congress (ANC) decided to suspend armed conflict. This was a response to the Pretoria government's clear willingness to come to a peace agreement, signalled firstly in President F. W. de Klerk's speech on 2 February 1990, by Nelson Mandela's release from prison nine days later, and by a meeting in Groote Schuur in May. Even so, the peace process remained a complex task, full of suspicions of duplicity on both sides.

As conflict between the ANC and the white government declined, it escalated between the ANC and the Inkatha Freedom Party. Led by Chief Buthelezi, the Inkatha was partly funded and equipped by government agents. That conflict lasted until the elections in 1994.

## 32 KEEPING PEACE

The lesson of the UN peacekeeping operations, whose bare outlines are sketched on this map, is that they can succeed if and only if two conditions are met. Firstly, there has to be a peace to keep. Secondly, the necessary resources have to be available. If there is no peace to keep, the UN Blue Helmets can only stand by and watch the fighting. From Bosnia, via southern Lebanon to Somalia – and in the early 1960s also in Zaire – experience shows that peacekeeping troops on the ground are no substitute for a political solution, and no means of achieving one either. If there are inadequate resources, then, as in Angola, the UN forces risk losing sight of events in localities far away from their headquarters or the national capital. What they cannot monitor, they have no chance of controlling. And resources are more than money and people: in Bosnia-Herzegovina, the mandate – or mission – extended far beyond peacekeeping to include protection of designated safe areas, but the UN forces were not given the equipment, the numbers or the detailed rules of engagement (instructions about circumstances in which they may open fire) that could make a reality of that mandate.

In some operations, serious and tragic mistakes have been made by UN forces. This has been best documented in the case of operations in Bosnia-Herzegovina, where UN forces were not only under great pressure but also under the closest media scrutiny. Many actions and cases of inaction that were castigated by the Bosnian government and by the international news media – such as when Dutch troops were unable to prevent the Bosnian Serb occupation of Srebrenica and the subsequent massacres – were the result, not of misjudgement by troops and officers, but of the situation created by political decisions in the UN Security Council. But there were also incidents that cannot be understood in that way. What may have been the lowest point was reached relatively early in the war in January 1993, when French UN troops who were transporting Bosnian Deputy Prime Minister Hakija Turajlic stopped for a Serb checkpoint in Sarajevo. Serb soldiers looked in the vehicle and, recognizing Turajlic, shot and killed him.

Despite such incidents, the fashionable habit of blaming the UN for everything that goes wrong in some high profile operations is misleading. It ignores everything that goes well and puts the blame in the wrong place. The key decisions are taken in the UN Security Council, where power is shared by five states, the permanent members: China, France, Russia, the UK and the USA. Their policies drive UN operations forward, fuelled more by the need of their leaders to satisfy a domestic political constituency than by a determination to resolve the complexities of peace.

The map presents a somewhat different tally of UN operations from those in official UN documents and summaries. This is because I have deliberately ignored any distinction between operations in the same place if UN forces were carrying out the same mission. I have also ignored bureaucratic distinctions, put troops and police together and sidestepped the technical distinction between peacekeeping and observer missions.

## 33 FORCING PEACE

In 1992, when ambitions and optimism for the UN's Blue Helmet forces were at their height, Secretary-General Boutros Boutros Ghali wrote a report arguing that the UN should expand its role in peacemaking. Whereas the UN had hitherto concentrated on 'peacekeeping' after a peace agreement had been reached (see **32 Keeping Peace**), he now proposed 'peace enforcement'. That is, he argued that the UN could force warring parties to come to the negotiating table. The idea of peace enforcement is that when the killing stops, the underlying problems can then be sorted out. Its weakness is that warring parties can be forced to negotiate but they cannot be forced to want peace.

The major powers have been reluctant to let UN Blue Helmet forces go into action with the equipment and the rules of engagement (covering when they may open fire) appropriate for peace enforcement. There seems to be a fear that this could pave the way to the world organization maintaining a large permanent force that would ultimately jeopardize their national sovereignty. Peace enforcement has, however, been attempted with the backing of international organizations such as NATO, the Commonwealth of Independent States and the Economic Organization of West African States. At the end of the day, the results have been just as mixed as for UN peacekeeping forces.

This map includes a variety of kinds of operations, not all of which would qualify for peace enforcement in the sense of forcing warring parties to the negotiating table. The force in Egypt, for example, is deployed in the Sinai to ensure compliance with the disengagement treaty between Egypt and Israel. That is a classic peacekeeping mission. What this force has in common with all the others on the map is that those who carry them out claim some kind of international authorization for the operations, but even if the legitimacy comes from the UN, they are not conducted as UN Blue Helmet missions.

Much of the research for this map was by Pavel Baev.

## 34 MAKING PEACE

There are two main problems in providing information on efforts at conflict resolution by independent organizations. The first is that many of the organizations seek to protect the confidentiality of the process. Premature publicity is rarely helpful and often destructive. They may, therefore, prefer not to talk in public about what they are doing, and often even deny that they are doing it. The second problem is far less creditable, though it is also – thankfully – less common. For there are a few organizations who, far from shunning publicity, court it and exaggerate their role so that they can raise money. Indeed, a few organizations call almost any activity conflict resolution.

I have left off this map various activities that I know about but whose confidentiality I thought it right to maintain. For the rest, I have taken a broad view of the kind of activities that contribute to conflict resolution. I have included negotiations, seminars, training weeks and weekends, contact meetings, roundtable discussions, one or two apparently scholarly activities such as academic conferences and even some film making, when these activities involve direct or indirect representatives of conflict parties or could help strengthen the local capacity to resist the logic of conflict.

In the colours on the map, I have introduced a new category – political violence. This means lethal violence that is politically motivated but is not armed conflict, either because it is not centrally organized or because there is no continuity between clashes. Rioting and looting are examples of the kind of violence that might be included under this heading. The countries in which there is this political violence, short of armed conflict, are cases in which early conflict resolution could prevent further escalation to war.

The Norwegian research institute that helped establish the 1993 Oslo 'back channel' between Israel and the Palestine Liberation Organization is known by the acronym of FAFO, which translates as the Institute for Applied Social Science.

## TABLE OF WARS 1990-95

The shape of armed conflicts today (see **1 The Red Horse**) makes the task of classifying and counting them surprisingly complex. Researchers who monitor armed conflicts globally produce very different estimates. The group whose approach is closest to my own is based in the Department of Peace and Conflict Research at Uppsala University, Sweden. They identify 35 armed conflicts in 1995; I identify 55.

Some of the discrepancy lies in the definitions and some in the attitude to the sources of information. The definition of war that I use is that it consists of:
• open armed conflict
• about power or territory
• involving centrally organized fighters and fighting
• with continuity between clashes.
(One small point of terminology: because war is armed conflict, I use these two terms interchangeably; some researchers limit the term 'war' to the bigger armed conflicts.)

The most important difference between this and some other definitions is that I do not include a phrase such as 'involving the forces of a recognized government of a state on at least one side of the conflict.' This is a change from previous editions of this atlas. The reason for the change is that in Somaliland and Kurdistan, fighting has gone on during the 1990s on a scale and of a type that is absolutely the same as what we normally call war, but without the recognized government being involved. A definition based on the participation of a recognized government would also be misleading in the case of countries where real governmental authority has collapsed, such as Liberia or Somalia in the 1990s and Lebanon in the 1980s.

Like other researchers, I use a low threshold of casualties. The lower limit is 25 war deaths in any one year, in a conflict in which total war deaths number at least several hundred. The reason for this very low minimum figure is the common pattern of wars in which the level of activity goes through a series of peaks and troughs. The latter come when the insurgent forces withdraw from combat, if they can, to regroup, rethink and recruit. A year or two can go by in which there is relatively little activity, followed by a renewed burst of violence at a much higher level. It seems to me to be arbitrary and misleading to decide that the intervening period of relative inactivity was peace. At the same time, the period of low level activity seems to me only to qualify for the term armed conflict or war if it is in the context of a longer conflict in which the death toll is higher.

Attentive readers will notice some differences of presentation of various conflicts between this table and some of the maps. This is because there are different possibilities in the presentation of data, depending on the form used and the choices one makes about what to emphasize. One example is that in **21 The Horn of Poverty**, Sudan is shown as being at war from 1955 to 1972 and  again since 1983, while the table shows one war lasting since 1955. This was essentially the same war with a decade of peace in the middle. It is one example of the way in which the presentation of data on the maps allowed a closer look than is always possible in a summary table whose main objective is to make it possible to grasp a complex reality. On the other hand, fighting in Burma is presented in some detail in **16 After the Raj** and in this table, but is presented as one undifferentiated conflict in **22 Islands of Conflict**. In **31 Lands of Good Hope**, I have shown the 1990 peace agreement between the ANC and the apartheid government, whereas in the table, armed conflict is shown as lasting until 1994, which it did, but between the ANC and the Inkatha Freedom Party. These are examples of the choices I have made about where to place the emphasis.

The table records the status of wars up to the end of 1995. It includes every armed conflict that was active at any point between the beginning of 1990 and the end of 1995. Because wars often stop for a while and start up again, I have used the concept of combat being 'suspended'. For conflicts that appear to have been suspended without an agreement – possibly because at least one of the parties is simply exhausted – I have used the concept of 'a decisive break in action.' After a period, however, the break may not look so decisive. If the list were extended to include armed conflicts in 1996, the conflict between Nigeria and Cameroon over territorial issues in the Bakassi border region would be amongst those added.

Ajami, Fouad, *The Arab Predicament*, Cambridge: Cambridge University Press, 1992.

Allard, Kenneth, *Somalia Operations: Lessons Learned*, Washington D.C.: National Defence University Press, 1995.

Allison, Roy, *Peacekeeping in the Soviet Successor States*, Chaliot Paper no.18, Paris: Institute for Security Studies WEU, 1994.

Amer, Ramses, *Peace-keeping in a Peace Process: The Case of Cambodia*, Report no. 40, Uppsala: Department of Peace and Conflict, Uppsala University, 1995.

Amnesty International, *Amnesty International Annual Report*, 1992 to 1995, London: Amnesty International.

Asmus, Ronald D., Richard L. Kugler and F. Stephen Larrabee, NATO expansion: the next steps, *Survival*, vol. 37 no. 1, spring 1995, pp.7-33.

Asmus, Ronald D., Robert D. Blackwill and F. Stephen Larrabee, Can NATO survive? *The Washington Quarterly*, vol. 19 no. 2 spring 1996, pp.79-101.

Aung San Suu Kyi, *Current Biography*, February 1992.

Ayubi, Nazih. *Political Islam: Religion and Politics in the Arab World*, London: Routledge, 1991.

Baev, Pavel, *The Russian Army in a Time of Troubles*, London: Sage, 1996.

Barraclough, Geoffrey, ed., *The Times Atlas of World History*, 6th edition, London: Times Books, 1984.

Barrat Brown, Michael and Pauline Tiffen, *Short Changed: Africa and World Trade*, London: Pluto Press, 1992.

Barrat Brown, Michael, *Africa's Choices*, London: Penguin, 1995.

Boahen, A. Adu, ed., *General History of Africa: VII Africa under Colonial Domination 1880-1935*, abridged edition, London: James Currey; Paris: United Nations Educational, Scientific and Cultural Organization, 1990.

Boutros Ghali, Boutros, *An Agenda for Peace*, New York: United Nations, 1992.

Boyle, Kevin and Tom Hadden, The peace process in Northern Ireland, *International Affairs*, vol. 71 no. 2, 1995. pp.269-83.

Brogan, Patrick, *World Conflicts*, 2nd edition, London: Bloomsbury, 1992.

Burgat, Francois & William Dowell, *The Islamic Movement in North Africa*, Texas: Center for Middle Eastern Studies at the University of Texas at Austin, 1993.

Böge, Volker, *Bougainville: A 'Classical' Environmental Conflict?* Environment and Conflicts Project (ENCOP) Occasional Paper no.3, Zurich: Centre for Security Studies and Conflict Research; Bern: Swiss Peace Foundation,1992.

Carter Center, *International Guide to NGO Activities in Conflict Prevention and Resolution*, Atlanta, Ga: Carter Center, December 1995.

Cawthra, Gavin, *Brutal Force: The Apartheid War Machine*, London: International Defence & Aid Fund for Southern Africa, 1986.

Central Intelligence Agency, *The World Factbook 1994*, Washington D.C.: Central Intelligence Agency, 1994.

Centre for Defence Studies, *International Security Digest*, successive issues, 1990-95.

Chossudovsky, Michel, IMF-World Bank policies and the Rwandan holocaust, *Third World Resurgence*, no.52, 1994.

Cook, Chris and John Stevenson, *The Atlas of Modern Warfare*, London: Weidenfeld & Nicolson, 1978.

Copson, Raymond W., *Africa's Wars and Prospects for Peace*, New York: M.E. Sharpe, 1994.

Cook, Helena, *The Safe Haven in Northern Iraq: International Responsibility for Iraqi Kurdistan*, Essex: Human Rights Centre, University of Essex; London: Kurdistan Human Rights Project, 1995.

*Croatia, the Republic of, and the Republic of Bosnia & Hercegovina: A Concise Atlas*, Zagreb: The Miroslav Krleza Lexicographical Institute, 1993.

Crossman, Richard, *The Diaries of a Cabinet Minister*, vol. III, London: Hamish Hamilton, 1977.

Davidson, Basil, *Africa in History*, 4th edition, London: Paladin, 1984.

Davis, Anthony, The Conflict in Kashmir, *Jane's Intelligence Review*, vol. 7 no.1, 1995.

Delanty, Gerard, Negotiating the peace in Northern Ireland, *Journal of Peace Research*, vol. 32 no.3, August 1995.

Doyle, Michael W, *UN Peacekeeping in Cambodia: UNTAC's Civil Mandate*, International Peace Academy Occasional Paper, Boulder, Co: Lynne Rienner, 1995.

Findlay, Trevor, *Cambodia: The Legacy and Lessons of UNTAC*, SIPRI Research Report no. 9, Oxford: Oxford University Press, 1995.

Foss, Christopher and Terry J. Gander, *Jane's Military Vehicles and Ground Support Equipment*, 8th edition, London: Jane's Publishing, 1987.

Freedom House, *Freedom in the World: Annual Survey of Political Rights and Civil Liberties 1994-95*, New York: Freedom House, 1995.

Ganzel, Klaus Jurgen and Torsten Schwinghammer, *Die Kriege nach dem zweiten Weltkrieg 1945 bis 1992*, Munster: Lit, 1995.

Gèrard, Andrée, ed., *Clés pour l'Islam: du religieux au politique. Des Origines aux enjeux d'aujourd'hui*, Brussels: Institut de Récherche et d'Information sur la Paix et la Sécurité: GRIP, 1993.

Glenny, Misha, *The Fall of Yugoslavia*, London, Penguin: 1992.

Goldblat, Jozef, *Arms Control*, London: Sage Publications, 1994.

Government of Papua New Guinea, *Response by the Papua New Guinea Government to the United Nations Commission on Human Rights' Resolution on Alleged Human Rights Violation on Bougainville Province of Papua New Guinea*, 23 September 1994.

Gubarev, Vladimir, War on the 'Roof of the World', *Moscow News*, no.33, 13 August 1993.

Guelke, Adrian, Paramilitaries, Republicans and Loyalists, in Seamus Dunn, ed., *Facets of the Conflict in Northern Ireland*, London: Macmillan, 1995.

Gurr, Ted Robert, *Minorities at Risk*, Washington, D.C.: United States Institute of Peace, 1993.

Harkavy, Robert E., *Bases Abroad: The Global Foreign Military Presence*, Stockholm: Stockholm International Peace Research Institute; London: Oxford University Press, 1989.

Hersh, Seymour M., On the nuclear edge, *The New Yorker*, 29 March 1993, pp.56-73.

Hill, Fiona, *Russia's Tinderbox: Conflict in the North Caucasus and its Implications for the Future of the Russian Federation*, Harvard University, Cambridge, Ma: Strengthening Democratic Institutions Project, 1995.

Hill, Hall ed., *Unity and Diversity: Regional Economic Development in Indonesia since 1970*, Singapore: Oxford University Press, 1991.

Holland, R.F., *European Decolonization 1918-1981*, London: Macmillan, 1985.

Horowitz, Donald L., *Ethnic Groups in Conflict*, Berkeley, Ca: University of California Press, 1985.

Hunter, Brian, *Statesman's Yearbook 1994-1995*, 131st edition, London: Macmillan, 1994.

Ignatieff, Michael, Alone with the Secretary-General, *The New Yorker*, 14 August 1995.

International Committee of the Red Cross (ICRC), *Landmines and Blinding Weapons*, Press Documentation September 1995, Geneva: International Committee of the Red Cross, 1995.

International Federation of Red Cross and Red Crescent Societies, *World Disasters Report 1995*, Dordrecht: Martinus Nijhoff, 1995.

International Institute of Strategic Studies, *The Military Balance*, London: International Institute of Strategic Studies, annual.

International Institute for Strategic Studies, *Strategic Survey*, successive editions 1990-95, London: International Institute for Strategic Studies; Oxford University Press.

Islam, a survey, *The Economist* (London), 6 August 1994.

Israel. Central Bureau of Statistics, *Statistical Abstract of Israel*, Jerusalem: Central Bureau of Statistics, 1992.

Israel. Central Bureau of Statistics, *Information on 1995 census statistics*, Oslo: Embassy of Israel.

Israel. Ministry of Foreign Affairs, *Agreement on the Gaza Strip and the Jericho Area, May 4, 1994*, Jerusalem: Ministry of Foreign Affairs, 1994.

Izad, Mehrdad R., *The Kurds: A Concise Handbook*, Washington D.C.: Taylor and Francis, 1992.

Jane's Information Group, *Jane's Intelligence Review Yearbook: The Year in Conflict 1994-95*, Surrey: Jane's Information Group, 1994.

Jongman, A.J., Contemporary conflicts: a global survey of high and lower intensity conflicts and serious disputes, in *PIOOM Newsletter and Progress Report*, The PIOOM Foundation, vol. 7 no. 1, winter 1995.

Jonson, Lena and Clive Archer, eds., *Peacekeeping and the Role of Russia in Eurasia*, Boulder, Co: Westview Press, 1996.

*Keesings Record of World Events*, vols. 36-42 (1990-96) Harlow: Longman; Avenel: Cartermill, monthly.

Kelley, Kevin. *The Longest War: Northern Ireland and the IRA*, 2nd edition, London: Zed Books, 1988.

Kerr, Donald, *World Directory of Defence & Security*, London: Cartermill, 1995.

Kohn, George C., *Dictionary of Wars*, New York: Doubleday, 1987.

Krieger, Joel ed., *The Oxford Companion to Politics of the World*, New York: Oxford University Press, 1993.

Lintner, Bertil, Fall-out in the South Pacific, *Jane's Intelligence Review*, January 1996, pp.34-40.

Little, Alan and Lauren Silber, *Yugoslavia: Death of a Nation*, New York: Penguin, 1995.

Macrae, Joanna and Anthony Zwi, eds., *War and Hunger: Rethinking International Responses to Complex Emergencies*, London: Zed Books; UK Save the Children, 1994.

McDowall, David, *The Kurds, A Nation Denied*, London: Minority Rights Group, 1992.

*Middle East Peace Process: An Overview*, Jerusalem: Israeli Ministry of Foreign Affairs, 1995.

Minority Rights Group, *World Directory of Minorities*. Harlow: Longman, 1990.

Moser-Puangsuwan, Yeshua, UN peacekeeping in Cambodia: whose needs were met? *Pacifica Review*, vol. 7, no.2, 1995, pp.103-27.

Nilsen, Thomas, Storage of the Northern Fleet's nuclear waste, *Bellona Magazine*, no. 6 December 1995, pp.7-9.

Nilsen, Thomas and Nils Bøhmer, *Sources of Radioactive Contamination in Murmansk and Arkhangelsk Counties*, Oslo: Bellona Foundation Report no.1, 1994.

Nilsen, Thomas, Igor Kudrik and Aleksander Nikitin, *Zapadnaja Litsa*. Oslo: Bellona Foundation Working Paper, November 1995.

Norris, Robert S., French and Chinese nuclear weapon testing, *Security Dialogue* 1996, vol. 27 no. 1, pp. 39-54.

Northern Ireland Statistics and Research Agency, Census data 1995, March 1996, Belfast.

Okolo, J.E., and T.M. Shaw, eds., *The Political Economy of Foreign Policy in ECOWAS*, London: Macmillan, 1994.

Osaghae, Eghosa E., The Ogoni uprising: oil politics, minority agitation and the future of the Nigerian state, *African Affairs*, vol. 94 (1995), pp.325-344.

Owen, David, *Balkan Odyssey*, New York: Harcourt Brace, 1995.

Pakenham, Thomas, *The Scramble for Africa*, London: Weidenfeld & Nicolson, 1991.

Percival, Valerie and Thomas Homer-Dixon, *Environmental Scarcity and Violent Conflict: The Case of Rwanda*, University of Toronto, 1995.

Physicians for Human Rights, *Landmines, a Deadly Legacy*, The Arms Project, Physicians for Human Rights, New York: Human Rights Watch, 1993.

Poulton, Hugh, *The Balkans*, London: Minority Rights Group, 1991.

Raevsky, A. and I.N. Vorob'ev, *Russian Approaches to Peacekeeping Operations*, UNIDIR Research Paper no.28, Geneva: United Nations Institute for Disarmament Research, 1994.

Richards, Paul, Rebellion in Liberia and Sierra Leone: a crisis of youth? in Oliver Furley, ed., *Conflict in Africa*. London: I.B. Tauris, 1994.

Roberts, Shawn and Jody Williams, *After the Guns Fall Silent: The Enduring Legacy of Landmines*, Washington D.C: Vietnam Veterans of America Foundation, 1995.

Seton-Watson, Hugh, *Nations and States*, London: Methuen, 1982.

Shermatova, Sanobar, Who with whom and for what is fighting in Tajikistan, *Moskovskie Novosti*, no. 6, 11-18 February 1996. (In Russian.)

Shivers, Lynne and David Bowman. *More than the Troubles: A Common Sense View of the Northern Ireland Conflict*. Philadelphia, Pa: New Society Publishers, 1984.

Simensen, Jarle, *Afrikas historie - nye perspektiver*, 2nd edition, Oslo: J.W. Cappelen a.s.,1990.

Singh, Jasjit, ed., *Light Weapons and International Security*, Delhi: Indian Pugwash Society & British American Security Information Council, 1995.

Steele, Jonathan, *Eternal Russia*, London, Faber & Faber, 1995.

Stockholm International Peace Research Institute, *World Armaments & Disarmament: SIPRI Yearbook 1985*, London: Taylor & Francis, 1985.

Stockholm International Peace Research Institute, *SIPRI Yearbook*, successive years 1990-95, New York: Oxford University Press.

Tatevosyan, Ara and Vladimir Emelyanenko, Bosnian implacability of Karabakh, *Moskovskie Novosti*, no.8, 25 February - 3 March, 1996. (In Russian.)

United Nations, *Annexes to the Final Report of the United Nations Commission of Experts, New York, Document S/1994/674: Annex IX Rape and Sexual Assault; Annex X Mass Graves*, New York: UN, December 1994.

United Nations, *The Blue Helmets: A Review of United Nations Peace-keeping*, 2nd edition, New York: UN Department of Public Information, 1990.

United Nations, *The United Nations and Cambodia*, New York: UN Department of Public Relations, 1995.

United Nations, *The United Nations and Mozambique*, New York: UN Department of Public Relations, 1995.

United Nations, *UN Peacekeeping: Information Notes*, December 1994, New York: UN Department of Public Information, 1994.

United Nations Conference on Trade and Development, *Handbook of International Trade and Development Statistics*, Geneva: United Nations Publications 1993.

United Nations Development Programme, *Human Development Report 1994*, New York: Oxford University Press, 1994.

United Nations Development Programme, *Human Development Report 1995*, New York: Oxford University Press, 1995.

UNICEF, *State of the World's Children 1996*, New York: Oxford University Press, 1996.

United Nations Relief and Works Agency for Palestine Refugees in the Near East (UNRWA), information on refugee and general population numbers, 8 September 1995, Vienna: UNWRA. Personal communication.

US Committee for Refugees, *World Refugee Survey*, successive years 1990-95, Washington D.C.: US Committee for Refugees.

US Committee for Refugees, preliminary data to be published in: *1996 World Refugee Survey*, Washington D.C.: US Committee for Refugees, 1996.

US. Department of State, *Patterns of Global Terrorism*, successive years 1990-95, Washington D.C.: Department of State Publications.

US. Office of International Security and Peacekeeping Operations, *Hidden Killers: The Global Problem with Uncleared Landmines*, 1993 Report on International Demining, Washington D.C.: US State Department, 1993.

US. Office of International Security and Peacekeeping Operations, *Hidden Killers: The Global Landmine Crisis*, 1994 report to the US Congress, Washington D.C.: US State Department, 1994.

University of Bradford, *International Peacekeeping News*, vol. 1 issues 9-11, 1995.

Vulliamy, Ed, *Seasons in Hell*, London: Simon & Schuster, 1994.

Walton, John and David Seddon, *Free Markets & Food Riots*, Cambridge Ma.: Blackwell, 1994.

Wallensteen, Peter and Margareta Sollenberg, After the Cold War: emerging patterns of armed conflict 1989-94, *Journal of Peace Research*, vol. 32 no. 3, August 1995, pp. 345-60.

Water in the Middle East, *The Economist* (London), 23 December 1995 - 5 January 1996.

Welch, David A. and Odd Arne Westad, eds., *The Intervention in Afghanistan and the Fall of Détente*, Oslo: The Norwegian Nobel Institute, 1996.

Whose water? *The Economist* (London), 5 August 1995.

Williams, William Appleman et al, eds., *America in Vietnam*, New York: Doubleday, 1985.

Wilkie, James W., *Statistical Abstract of Latin America*, Los Angeles: UCLA Latin American Center Publications, 1995.

Wilkinson, Paul, Terrorist targets and tactics: new risks to world order, in Alison Jamieson, ed., *Terrorism and Drug Trafficking in the 1990s*, Vermont: Dartmouth, 1994.

Wilson, John, Observations on peacekeeping and peacemaking in the former Yugoslavia, in Hugh Smith, ed., *International Peacekeeping: Building on the Cambodian Experience*, Canberra: Australian Defence Studies Centre, 1994.

Wilson, Tom, *Ulster: Conflict and Consent*, Oxford: Basil Blackwell, 1989.

Whittaker, David J., *UN in Action: UN and Cambodia*, London:

University College London Press, 1995.

World Bank, *The World Bank Atlas 1995*, Washington D.C.:
World Bank, 1994.

World Bank, *World Development Report*, Washington D.C.:
World Bank, 1995.

World Bank, *World Debt Tables, 1994-1995*, Washington D.C.:
World Bank, 1995.


Journals:

*Africa Confidential*, 1990-95 (London).

*Africa Research Bulletin*, 1994-96 (Oxford).

*Africa Watch/Asia Watch/Americas Watch/Human Rights Watch*,
1994-96 (London).

*Caribbean and Central American Report*, 1995-96 (Guatemala City).

*Economist Intelligence Unit*, 1994-96 (London).

*East Timor Link*, 1995 (London).

*Far Eastern Economic Review*, 1994-96 (Hong Kong).

*Horn of Africa Bulletin*, 1993-96 (Uppsala).

*Jane's Intelligence Review*, 1990-95 (Surrey).

*Latin America Press*, 1995-96 (Lima).

*Middle East International*, 1990-96 (London).

*War Report*, 1991-96.(London).


Also:

Press and press agency reports.

Central Statistical Bureaus in OECD countries.

The RAND/ St. Andrews Chronology of International Terrorism.

United Nations Department of Humanitarian Affairs,
Land Mine Database, October 1995.

This index lists countries and topics appearing in the regional maps and given particular emphasis in the global maps. It covers the Notes (pages 97-119) but not the **Table of Wars 1990-95** (pages 90-95).